# 1001 WAYS
# TO BEAT THE TIME TRAP

# 1001 WAYS
## TO BEAT THE TIME TRAP

### WILLIAM J. BOND

**FREDERICK FELL PUBLISHERS, INC.**
NEW YORK, NEW YORK

For information address:
FREDERICK FELL PUBLISHERS, INC.
386 Park Avenue South
New York, New York 10016

Library of Congress Catalog Card Number: 81-68915
International Standard Book Number: 0-8119-0441-5

MANUFACTURED IN THE UNITED STATES OF AMERICA
1  2  3  4  5  6  7  8  9  0

Published simultaneously in Canada by
Fitzhenry & Whiteside, Limited, Toronto

# CONTENTS

# 1001 WAYS
# TO BEAT THE TIME TRAP

IN ORDER TO DO your job more efficiently, to manage your time better, you must look closely at the time allotted to you. Do you use it correctly? You are given the same amount as each person in your office, as much as your competitors, as much as your future competitors. Let's explore ways to make your time count. Time management requires your full attention to the jobs and assignments you take for yourself each day.

In a recent Time Management Seminar, I talked about the person who takes on too many jobs and assignments. When you have too many irons in the fire the quality of your work may suffer; you may find yourself suffering from the physical effects of doing too much work. One gentleman in the seminar felt that talking about how to use time helped him, because now instead of just taking on all the work in sight, he takes the necessary time to determine if he needs to do the work himself, or if it can be handled by others. (This gentleman, like many other managers, felt that along with the responsibility for the work in his department, he must overwork to be personally sure that all work is completed correctly and on time.)

Break your bad habits. Time management is the result of habits—good habits of making the best use possible of your time. Many managers find that lack of time is a real problem because they cannot find enough time to accomplish their goals and objectives. The bad habits, like taking on work that should be handled by others, can steal valuable minutes and hours of your time. Failing to plan your time carefully can consume your valuable time. Overextending yourself can be another bad habit you must break in order to reach your goals. You can change, you can convert many of those bad habits into good habits to help you succeed. Here are a number of ways to help you.

# 1
# DIVIDING UP
# YOUR TIME

One very basic way to look at your time is to divide it in three ways: your work time, your personal time, and your sleep time. Each person handles each time division in a different manner. One person will split her time in thirds, about eight hours a day for work, eight hours for personal life, and the remaining time for sleep. Another person will spend twelve hours at work, two hours for personal life, and ten hours for sleep. Still another person might find that he needs twelve hours of sleep, and spends the remaining twelve hours at work. There is no time left for personal life, and this is just the way this individual wants it.

A housewife in Ohio, Lois V., felt her time was divided in two separate units: one unit of time was called OURS, time she devoted for the family, which included cooking, washing, cleaning, keeping the children's activities and transportation organized, and numerous other activities for the family. Another unit was called MY time in which she could do things she wanted to do completely for herself. These activities included getting her hair done, going to lunch with her girl friends, and going to the library to review the latest books in her favorite field of interior design. Many psychologists claim that each day you should do something that you enjoy. Be selfish if you must. Try to do something in which you get satisfaction or look forward to doing. Is your day filled with OURS items? How many

MY items do you have each day? Do you have enough MY items to keep you happy?

Lois V. found that in order to reach her new goals to become a certified interior designer, she had to arrange her time schedule so that more time was devoted to MY items, and with the help of asking other mothers to start car pools for the children, and hiring a capable baby sitter, she turned toward the completion of the MY items. She started night school for a few introductory courses in the interior design field. Once she successfully completed these courses she decided to start and finish the program during the day. This was a difficult process for Lois, but she found that thinking about the MY items made her all the more determined. She found herself thinking of new and easier ways to reach out and tackle the MY items. Each time she would complete a MY item, such as a college course or a floor plan assignment for a commercial building, it would build her confidence for more and larger MY items. She also found that during the time of these MY accomplishments she found new areas of interests with her husband. He offered support and gave her help in some of her OURS items. Looking back on this period in her life, the only regret Lois expressed was simply, "I only wish I reviewed my use of my time. I had the feeling that the OURS items belonged only to me. I never realized that a great deal of people including my husband could also contribute to doing them." Lois built not only her inner confidence in herself, but also management skills, in supervising the OUR items to be certain all these items were done correctly and on time.

Just as Lois developed her own time management that met her own needs, you can also develop a program in your job to help you accomplish the more important items. Bill N. had a real problem as an office manager in a medium-sized manufacturing company. He worked later and later each night, and worked a full day on Saturday to finish his work. In a full time check to see where he was spending his time, he found that a large part of each day was devoted to reports he gave to his boss, the treasurer of the company. Another large block of time each day was concerned with reports for the company, such as payroll reports, filing the tax reports, processing invoices, and sending out invoices. Once he accomplished the work for his boss, and then the work for the company, he had very little time to accomplish his own projects that he felt were important for the company. Bill N. wanted to fully computerize the accounting system to save him time and money for his company.

In order to fully see the problem he was facing, Bill wrote the word MOB on his desk pad. M stood for MY, the jobs and assignments that he wanted to accomplish. O stood for the OUR items, the routine but important jobs like payroll and internal reports so very important to keep the company running successfully and smoothly. B stood for the reports, jobs, and tasks he handled for the boss. He made sure that the boss received all this information on time and completely accurate. Bill looked at his time scheduling problem just like he would look at other management problems, taking each part of the problem and seeing if something could be eliminated or changed. He continued to try to describe the problem in one complete sentence to help solve it. Over and over in his mind he talked it out. "How can I spend more time on MY items? The OUR and BOSS items are consuming too much of my time. There is a better way. I want to find it."

The answer finally came to Bill one evening when he woke up from a sound sleep. It was about three o'clock in the morning and the idea came directly to him. You can solve your time problems by spending more of your time on the MY items—especially the top MY item, a new computer system. With the new computer system, you can produce the reports and jobs for both your BOSS and for your OURS obligations. By concentrating on the MY top priority, the computer, it will then be able to do the work to help you in other areas such as the BOSS and OURS areas. Good time management means looking at all areas. In some cases, like Bill's, working on the B and O items showed that Bill was working harder but not necessarily smarter. He started to work smarter when he took the necessary time to ask himself, "Just where does my time go each day? What specifically can I do about it?" Just as the idea to solve the problem came in the middle of the night for Bill, make sure that when you have an evening that starts to pump ideas and solutions for you, that you take a pad of paper and write them down before you lose these very valuable ideas.

To succeed in your position at work, and to move up the ladder to the next rung in your career, you must complete new assignments to help your department and company increase their profits. Your supervisor or boss is happy to see you complete the B and O items, but he or she is more interested in extra items such as the new computerized accounting system, the new energy savings report, the new production analysis report, or the five-year report you promised eighteen months ago. You can spend a large amount of time and energy complaining about your workload and explaining why you cannot complete the extra work which is essential to your job, but it will be up to you, and you alone, to find a way to start and complete these MY jobs.

Just like Bill's example of finally finding the idea that worked for him, you will find the answer to your individual time problems by being persistent. Keep thinking about the problem. Even while you are presently struggling with the B and O items, keep your thinking tuned to your M's. Your MY items are in many ways the most important to you. For your M's to be successful you must also set them up in order of importance or priority. Which M is the most important at this time? Why is it important to you? What is the payoff for you? How will you reward yourself when you finally complete your MY item?

There are numerous ways to waste time during your valuable MY time. Some people use this time to see how other departments in the company are doing. Others get on the telephone to see how friends and associates are doing in their jobs and careers. One woman executive in a recent time management seminar thought a good amount of her time was consumed by drop-in visitors. Her biggest problem drop-in visitor happened to be her boss. Why not communicate to your boss that although you would like to continue to talk, you're presently working on a very top-priority item? The BOSS obligations are already completed.

Another member of the seminar, Harry A., thought too much

of his MY time was consumed by too many simple questions from assistants who were originally hired to help him. He needed all the time possible to concentrate on a very important MY time item: a five-year plan for the company. Completion of the five-year plan required a decision to spend less time with the assistants and more time on the five-year plan. Harry A. called in one of his top assistants, Sue B., and assigned her the responsibility of working with the other assistants. She would help them with their various day-to-day questions. Harry A. had wanted to make a move like this for a long time. The present situation forced him to make it now so that he could protect his MY time. How do you watch over your MY time? Do you permit other people or other problems to steal your valuable MY time? Take the example of Harry A. If he continued to permit his assistants to steal his time he would never finish the valuable projects and assignments which would help him get his promotions and opportunities to move up the ladder of success in the company.

Let's pretend instead that Harry A. failed to delegate the job of working with his assistants, and because of this he never reached back for the extra effort to complete the five-year plan or the other projects he promised himself with his MY time. So the day arrives finally when Harry A. sits down with his boss to review his performance for the year. Harry has worked hard all year long and now he looks forward to this very important meeting. During the review, the boss says to Harry, "Yes, I know you have made a real effort to do the work I assigned to you during the past year, and as far as I know you have handled the routine reports for the company. But Harry, I'm still waiting for the five-year report, and the data on the ABC account you promised me months ago. Quite frankly, Harry, I'm disappointed this important work is not finished by now."

Harry is quick to point out, "Now just wait a minute, boss. You know how hard I work to make sure you have all the reports and information you need. I also work many hours getting the company reports out on time. I cannot see why you're disappointed at all."

The boss expects this reply and promptly answers, "Harry, I hired you to manage. This includes your people, your machines, and your methods. I really don't care how you get the job done, just get it done."

This is an example of what could happen when you cannot get the full use of your MY time. You must determine what your top-priority job is, and then get started on it. What is the job that will give you the highest return on investment of your time? For the teacher, a very high-priority job is simply preparing for tomorrow's lessons. For the salesperson it might be to get five appointments to present the new products. For the manager of the accounting department a top priority might be to completely review all the financial statements before he or she presents them to the president. The secretary might find her top priority making an editorial change in the form letter for new customers. The supervisor in the production department may find his top priority is to get the number four machine fixed so that production can be kept at the maximum level. Another top priority might be to spend more time playing tennis, still another priority is to spend more time with your children and friends.

What is the top priority for tomorrow? Determining your top priority requires a number of steps and a certain amount of time to think it over carefully. Some excellent time managers find that they spend their commuting time thinking about what their top-priority item will be for the day. An executive in the computer business finds she spends three hours, from the time she gets up in the morning until the time she arrives at work, considering the top or top two or three priorities.

Shown on page 9 is a time management form I have prepared to help you zero in on your top priorities and help you protect your MY time. Now write down the things that you know you must do tomorrow and include everything that must be completed. Write down all of them—the routine as well as the more difficult items. At this stage, just list the items without consideration about priorities. Go ahead and list them, it's your book. Use it as a tool, and write in your book.

# Things to do Today

Date:_____

☐ 1 _____ ✓
☐ 2 _____ ☐
☐ 3 _____ ☐
☐ 4 _____ ☐
☐ 5 _____ ☐
☐ 6 _____ ☐
☐ 7 _____ ☐
☐ 8 _____ ☐
☐ 9 _____ ☐
☐ 10 _____ ☐
☐ 11 _____ ☐

**ILLUSTRATION 1.**

Let's say that you are a sales representative for a computer company, and your main job is to sell educational computers to elementary teachers. You have the New England territory and this particular day you are working in the Rutland, Vermont, area. On page 10 is a listing from Joan Clark's sales representative's records.

Now that you have written out the jobs that you must complete for tomorrow, think about the jobs that are the most important to you. What jobs will be the "high payoff"—the items that will give you the best return on your investment. Remember, you are selling your time and your ability to accomplish certain jobs each day. These jobs require your special skills, talents, and abilities. Take the necessary time to determine what is the number one priority, then consider what will be the number two priority, then consider what job will be the number three priority. In each seminar on time

Date. Jan. 15, 19—

# Things to do Today

☐ **1**   Call main sales office on Expense Check                    ✓☐

☐ **2**   Call sales manager on date for next meeting               ☐

☐ **3**   Make sales presentation #1 Elem. School, Rutland, VT    ☐

☐ **4**                           2   "      "         "      "     ☐

☐ **5**                           3   "      "         "      "     ☐

☐ **6**                           4   "      "         "      "     ☐

☐ **7**   Make four new appointments for the next time in          ☐

☐ **8**         the Rutland, VT area (approx. 2 months)            ☐

☐ **9**   Finish monthly sales report for main office              ☐

☐ **10**  Read new material on company products                    ☐

**ILLUSTRATION 2.**

management, I am asked how to determine what the most important priority will be. I quite frankly feel that it matters very little if you take one job as number one and another job as number two, as long as both jobs are important to you and your career. In setting priorities, I'm primarily speaking about priorities in the world of work. But these same exercises can be used for your personal life as well. Personal time management will be discussed in a later chapter. What is important to you? What do you really want to do? Not what someone else wants you to do, but what you really want to do. Your time is your own and you should spend it any way you like. The successful time managers have an ability to continue to pick a large number of "high payoff" items. Try to be persistent in picking important priorities. Do it each day, day in and day out.

Now go back to Illustration 1 and carefully look at all the jobs you wanted to accomplish for tomorrow. This will take you much longer than just the original listing of your jobs. Now you must determine what jobs are most important to you. Weigh their importance, then make your decision about the number one priority and write it on Illustration 3 on Page 13. Do the same for number two and number three, and so on until you have finished grading the total jobs. Now I'm sure that this is not really something new to you. You try to do this each day, but you do it more quickly, not fully weighing the value of each priority. Take a close look at your number one priority. Is it really an important priority? Can you hire someone else in your company to do it for you? Can you put your highest priority into a machine or in some way automate the completion of this job? Would you be willing to share your number one priority with your boss or your associates? Do you feel you can get a good return on your time invested from your top-priority items? Why? I think you can see that taking the necessary time to review the priorities you have picked as top priorities is not an easy task, but it can be very rewarding. Choosing your top priorities can give you the direction you need for the rest of the day.

Try not to give way to the natural reaction of setting up priorities that are filled with routine, easily delegated, or time-consuming items. You as one person can only know and accomplish so much. In order to realize your full potential, you may be required to cut your workload to accomplish your most important work. For example, in a recent time management seminar, I had my class write down, in no special order, jobs they knew they wanted to accomplish the next day at work. They filled out a list just like the one you just completed on Illustration 1. This listing consumed only a few minutes before completion. The next step, and the most important, was the completion of Illustration 3 on page 13—determining from the list of five or six jobs the most important job or priority listed on Illustration 1, on page 9. This required more time because they now had to determine which job was their "top" job. After a number of minutes the job of listing the highest-priority job was completed and the class seemed relieved. I then asked if any member of the seminar group was willing to share their choice for the number one priority.

One woman sitting in the front of the class raised her hand and said, "Tomorrow my number one priority will be to do the payroll to include raises voted on during the last union contract. It's very important that this is done correctly. I want to be completely involved in this payroll."

On the surface this sounded like an excellent priority. Many of the employees had been waiting for this payroll for a number of weeks. One gentleman in the back of the room wanted to be heard and I eagerly called on him. I expected that he wanted to share his top priority with the class. He said, "I want to talk about that top priority just mentioned regarding the payroll for the company. She keeps mentioning that *she* must do the work to be sure that the work is correct. How large or small is the company? Does she have other people working for her or is she the only member of the office? Why not delegate this priority to the person in charge of this work?"

The spotlight was then turned on the woman again. She quickly added that she is, in fact, in charge of the office and the person in charge of payroll could accomplish the work. The woman agreed that instead of doing the work herself, she would delegate that job to the payroll worker, and then go on to the next highest priority on her list. Delegating the job still means you must check to be certain that the work is completed correctly, and on time.

Do you find yourself spending more and more time on jobs that are routine and could be handled by others? Are they really and truly "high payoff" jobs? How long will it take you to train someone else to take on your routine work? Successful people mind their time in such a way to free themselves and go on to the even more important work for their own success in their businesses or careers.

Complete Illustration 3 on page 13 with jobs you determine you are unable to delegate, and which your valuable time is truly needed to complete. Move to the number one priority, then to the number two, in that manner. List them in order of their priority.

Now that you have completed Illustration 3, setting up your

Date:_____

# Things to do Today

| Immediate Action: | Completed: √ |
|---|---|
| ☐ 1 _____ | ☐ |
| ☐ 2 _____ | ☐ |
| ☐ 3 _____ | ☐ |
| ☐ 4 _____ | ☐ |
| ☐ 5 _____ | ☐ |
| ☐ 6 _____ | ☐ |
| ☐ 7 _____ | ☐ |
| ☐ 8 _____ | ☐ |
| ☐ 9 _____ | ☐ |
| ☐ 10 _____ | ☐ |

ILLUSTRATION 3.

own priorities for tomorrow, you are ready to start on your most important jobs. One very important word of caution: stay on that number one priority just as long as possible. You may find that you will spend four or five hours on this job. You may also find that at the end of the day you are still working on the most important job, so working late and for this length of time is fine.

Expect some problems to pop up along the way. One of my clients used the same technique we used in Illustrations 1 and 3 to help him in his selling job. Once he had his time plan completed, he went to work on it early the next day. He found a road block right away. He could not complete his number one priority because the customer was out of town. Now just as with any other plan, you must make the necessary adjustments. He then went on to his next priority and got back to the customer when he returned from his trip. Good time management is being able to roll with the punches, to make minor adjustments, but to get back on track when a top priority cannot be completed right away. While you're working on a top priority, you may find yourself thinking about a lower priority— to call another employee, or to set up a meeting, or to return a telephone call. Don't stop your top-priority job to do these lower level jobs, or you will end up consuming a great deal of time with the stop-and-start work style. If you cannot delegate these jobs to others within your office, take a five- or ten-minute break and take care of these small jobs. When these small jobs take more than the five or ten minutes you have set aside for them, drop them, and do them later.

Earlier in the book I talked about reviewing in an informal manner the time management techniques used by other people in your own home, your office, and other offices you come in contact with in your travels. How do your associates spend their time? How does your boss spend his or her time? Does he delegate enough work to you? Does he spend enough time on jobs that will help him get promoted to the next level?

Let's now look at how Joan Clark, the sales representative for educational computers, sets up her priorities. She listed these priorities on page 10, Illustration 2. On the following page you will find that she has listed her priorities in order of importance. This is very interesting. Notice that her number one priority is to make the four sales presentations to the various elementary schools in the Rutland, Vermont, area. Notice her number two priority, or the second highest priority, is to prepare herself for the next trip to the Rutland area by setting up other appointments in the middle of March. The third priority is to finish the sales report for the main sales office. The fourth priority is to call the sales office, and this gives her the opportunity to combine two jobs at the same time—asking about the date of the next sales meeting, and checking on the expense check.

In selling, the most important jobs is obviously to sell products or services. A company cannot stay in business unless it maintains sufficient sales to pay its bills, payroll, cost of products sold, and other operating costs. Joan Clark is correct in assigning the calls for sales as the top priority, and she should continue to give selling this very high priority. The important point in scheduling your time is to be consistent in your high payoff items. Stay on the important work.

We have now talked about the important elements in proper time management. First, listing your various jobs. Next, setting up priorities for completion of these jobs, while being aware that your time is divided into your work time, your personal time, and your sleep time. While working, you must concern yourself with MOB. The portion of your time that is called MY time will make the difference between accomplishing the goals and objectives you want to achieve. MY time is when your BOSS time and OUR time is completed, and it must be handled with care, nurtured, carefully

Date: Jan. 15, 19—

# Things to do Today

| Immediate Action: | | Completed: |
|---|---|---|
| ☐ 1 | Make sales presentation #1 Elem. School, Rutland, VT | ✓ ☐ |
| ☐ 2 | 2 " " " " | ☐ |
| ☐ 3 | 3 " " " " | ☐ |
| ☐ 4 | 4 " " " " | ☐ |
| ☐ 5 | Make 4 new appointments for the next time in | ☐ |
| ☐ 6 | the Rutland, VT area (approx. 2 months) | ☐ |
| ☐ 7 | Finish monthly sales report for main office | ☐ |
| ☐ 8 | Call sales manager on date for next meeting | ☐ |
| ☐ 9 | Call sales office on Expense Check | ☐ |
| ☐ 10 | Read new material on company products | ☐ |

ILLUSTRATION 4.

used, and never wasted on items that have a low priority, or are not important to you. You might start on your MY time at 4:30 P.M. in your job, or you might start this MY time at 10:00 A.M. in your job at home.

Stay on your guard to defend your MY time. There are numerous people, things, and activities that can steal, consume, and otherwise use up this amount of time. You may think that if you had more MY time you might accomplish more, but you must take the opportunity to manage all of your time, especially your MY time, and not let it manage you. MY time is important because once it begins it is all your own—no real deadlines, time deadlines, or closing dates, such as in the BOSS and OUR times. If you fail to get the job for your boss completed, he or she may get angry, and if this happens often enough your job may be in jeopardy. You want and need your job, so solving this problem will require your attention to the job in order to get it out on time. Your OUR time can also be a problem, but again, as with the BOSS time, you realize that these jobs and assignments are important for the good of the whole group, whether the group is your family, your office, or your company. The jobs in the OUR time are usually jobs that make the group run and work better together, and if the jobs are not completed on time, it will affect the group, or even slow the group down. Since neglecting to complete OUR time items on time will result in immediate reactions, usually negative, you will move to do these jobs on time. As you can see, the BOSS and OUR time items are usually done without delay.

The MY time must be managed so that you can get the most mileage from it. Try to ask yourself, "What is the most important job I can start when my MY time begins this afternoon? Can I at least start the ABC report? Why not finish the XYZ report on new product possibilities? Why not carefully look at the new production reports on the number three machine for last month?" Good use of your MY time requires proper thinking about the priorities of these jobs. How will you benefit from the completion of a particular job? Will your family benefit from your completion of a particular job? How will your company benefit from finishing a very difficult-to-complete job? Good time management results from carefully thinking about the beneficial results you can achieve by doing the work.

Try to make the priority exercises in Illustrations 1 and 3 an important part of your daily time control methods. Just as in any practice work, the more you do it the easier it will be to complete and work into your daily routine. Once you find yourself successfully using this method, it will become an important part of your time-management work style.

# 2
# GETTING MORE FROM YOUR TIME BY WATCHING THE TIME WASTERS

Do you manage your time? Many managers find that although they try their hardest to control and manage their time, the final result is too much work and too little time to accomplish it. Managers are paid to manage. You must manage your time in order to reach your career goals.

How do you manage your time? One of the best ways to start is to ask yourself these three simple questions:

1. Where should I spend my time?
2. What are my major time wasters?
3. How can I get more out of my time?

### Where Should You Spend Your Time?

Often managers run out of their valuable time because they "spread themselves too thin," simply trying to make everyone in the organization happy and trying to make all the small, medium, and large decisions within the company. In a recent time-management seminar a number of participants could not determine which task was the highest-priority task in their jobs. In order to answer this question you must consider the "high payoff" activities in your job.

Which activities are essential in your job? In order to manage your time you must separate the trivial and unimportant activities into the "high payoff" and important activities that will make or break your effectiveness.

Successful time managers have a very common characteristic: the ability to plan the activities for their workday and then follow their plan. Recent studies of office productivity showed that most workers reach their highest level of productivity around eleven o'clock in the morning and the peak starts to level off in the early afternoon. The first two hours in the morning could be used more effectively if the workers planned their workday more completely. One executive in a recent seminar said he spends two hours each morning just trying to determine what tasks are the most important for that particular day. The two hours are spent before he arrives in the office. By thinking about the tasks prior to getting to the office, he was ready to tackle them when he actually got there. He found himself visualizing in his own mind completing these jobs and feeling the sense of satisfaction of accomplishment. He would give himself a reward when he accomplished a number of tasks or an especially difficult one.

Develop time consciousness. Managers with time consciousness cannot waste time by doing a job the hard way, cannot permit themselves to perform work that could be handled faster and easier by an assistant or someone else within the office, and cannot tolerate antiquated methods and procedures that waste valuable time. Psychologists contend that nothing succeeds like success. When you find that by developing time consciousness you can produce work that you never felt was possible in the past, you will continue to use time successfully.

## What Are My Major Time Wasters?

Only you can answer this question. Just look around your office and you will find that certain employees use their time efficiently and get more work done. You will find many external time wasters, such as visitors and telephones which often steal some of your valuable time. The external time wasters come to you. You must deal with them to manage your time. For example, the social butterfly comes into your office to talk about the latest movie when you have a pile of urgent work to do. The internal time wasters must be managed by you. An example of an internal time waster is the lack of self-discipline or proper planning. The internal time wasters are your attitudes, your ability to develop a plan to use your time, your ability to stick to that plan, and your ability to specialize in a strong area. The time manager knows that unless he can discipline himself and his work, he will never be able to handle the external time wasters. By fully managing the internal time wasters you will be able to do the most productive thing possible at every given moment. Here are ten major time wasters:

## TEN MAJOR TIME WASTERS

| *External* | *Internal* |
|---|---|
| 1. Unplanned visitors | 1. Lack of proper priorities |
| 2. Unorganized meetings | 2. Too little delegation |
| 3. Excessive paperwork | 3. Spreading yourself too thin |
| 4. Poor communication | 4. Lack of an "I can do it" attitude |
| 5. Socializing | 5. Unclear planning |

The external time wasters can be controlled or eliminated if you discipline yourself and permit other workers to protect you from the external time wasters such as unplanned visitors and excessive paperwork. Let's look at the ten major time wasters one at a time.

# 3
# UNPLANNED VISITORS

Although you may not want to believe this, you can contribute to
the time waster taking a strong hold on your time. Let's take the first
external time waster, the *unplanned visitors* into your office. Why
do so many people come into your office to see you with their
problems? Not only the work-related problems, but the personal
problems as well. One woman at a time management seminar claimed
that her biggest time waster was the line of people trying to see her
about their personal problems. She admitted that she was more than
partly to blame. She had a personality that liked to help people by
giving them advice on how to handle their problems.

Unless you have a plan to handle the unplanned visitors, you
will have trouble spending your time on the work you know you
should be doing. If you permit these unplanned visitors to take your
precious time from you, the stack of unfinished work will still be
part of your job, and you will have less time to do it. As you move
up the ladder of success in your job, you will find yourself confronted
with more unplanned visitors because they feel that you now have
additional responsibility within the company, and they want to
spend more time with you. The first line of defense against the
unplanned visitors is to set aside a certain time of the day or the
week to see certain visitors such as salespeople, consultants, insurance agents, etc. One time manager from New York was forced

to set aside Thursday and Friday afternoons for seeing salespeople. A junior executive in Youngstown, Ohio, found that he cut down on his unplanned visitors when he demanded that they return at six o'clock in the evening to see him.

The second line of defense is to set guidelines with your secretary to stop unplanned visitors. A secretary can find the real purpose of the visitor's call and in many cases redirect the call to the right party. Good communications between you and your secretary can be extremely valuable in protecting your time. One secretary from Buffalo, New York, will ask an unplanned sales visitor the nature of his call. If she feels that her boss would like to talk to him in the future, she will say, "Mr. Bond is busy right now. Please leave one of your business cards, and if interested, he'll call you back." If you find that your secretary is permitting too many unplanned visitors to see you, new guidelines must be established to change this situation. A hospital in Boston found that many secretaries and doctors were interrupted by numerous people trying to find different offices, patient rooms, etc. A large sign was placed with clear instructions to the information desk. Once this sign was installed, the large volume of unplanned visitors dropped substantially.

Many unplanned visitors are your associates at work, your good friends, your spouses, your golfing buddies, and school chums. These special people will demand that you stop what you are presently doing to talk for a few minutes. When the personal conversation first starts out, you feel that it will only last for a few minutes, and then you can get back to your top priority. But the conversation often moves beyond the normal five minutes and will probably steal even more of your time. You have a choice. Just continue to feed the personal conversation, putting your top priority behind you and establishing a reputation as someone to see when personal problems arise, or take some action to save yourself. Here are just a few statements you could make to these time stealers:

- "Jack, I would like to talk about your situation further, but I must get a report out for my boss today."
- "Susan, although your situation is unique, my time is really

being stretched. The five-year plan is due soon. I must get back to it."

- "Mary, I'm busy right now, can I call you back to discuss it?"
- "I must go to a meeting in a few minutes. I must get ready for it."
- "I know that our conversation could go on for a longer period of time, but I have two other people waiting to see me with appointments."
- "Bill, sorry, but I must move on to other work. Let's set up a time to go to lunch together and discuss it."
- "Vicki, sorry, not right now. Let's discuss this after working hours."

Some of these statements are diplomatic, others are not. You must attempt to develop a reputation as someone who respects time and wants to make time count. You like people, but realize that you cannot solve all the personal problems in your office. You also set a good example for others by not wasting the valuable time of others. Your full concentration on the problem of unplanned visitors will help you deal successfully with them.

# 4
# UNORGANIZED MEETINGS

*Unorganized meetings* are major time wasters. Do you really need to attend these meetings? What do the meetings produce? Do you just attend these meetings or do you originate them? Can you get someone else in your office to attend these meetings and report on the important points of these meetings? A meeting should be called when it's absolutely necessary to call it for the good of the company. The real value of the meeting is to get feedback and ideas from various people within your department or your company. Sometimes the ideas developed and shared during a meeting can bring about a decision unavailable to the single decision-maker. In order to get the best information from your people in these meetings, you must plan ahead, introduce the subject of the meeting, run the meeting to facilitate full thinking and talking on the part of the others participating, keep it on track, stick to your agenda, and try to end the meeting on time.

A good time manager in Kokomo, Indiana, Joseph P., uses a meeting only when he feels that it's absolutely necessary, and then makes a plan of the meeting, carefully noting the problems and the main points of the meeting. This plan becomes the meeting agenda. Once the agenda is set, he then invites participants of the same rank and authority, giving them ample time to schedule their time for the meeting. His meetings last for ninety minutes, and he starts all meetings on time. Joseph P. has developed a reputation for starting on time, and because of this reputation his meetings have very few late participants. He also feels that the most important part of his meeting is the introduction of the problem, the real reason for the meeting. Once this is crystal clear to the participants it aids the overall success of the meeting. Joe sticks to his agenda, but he also tries to avoid giving his full solution to the problem. He tries to learn from the thoughts of the other participants. He tries hard to get ideas from all the participants. One idea from the shop supervisor in the machine shop will spur an idea from the office supervisor. Joe also summarizes during the meeting the general consensus of the different points on the agenda. He tries to end the meeting as soon as possible, carefully keeping to the ninety-minute termination timetable. Once the meeting is over, he then has the secretary type a copy of the minutes of the meeting and each participant gets a copy. Try to get the minutes of the meeting out as soon as possible, so that the participants of the meeting can see that their time and their ideas are being used well. Look around your company—what meetings do you enjoy, and why are the meetings so enjoyable? You might be able to use some of the same techniques in your own meetings.

Unorganized meetings result from the members being unprepared for the meeting. Too many meeting participants wait until the last minute before they start thinking about the main problem to be discussed in the meeting. One successful time manager sends a copy of the agenda to all participants before the meeting. Good participants in meetings are also good listeners. Give sufficient time to the views of others. One good technique is to take some notes of subjects you feel very confident to discuss and with your own sense of timing, give your views in the best delivery possible. Be careful that you keep your level of language on the level that all the participants can understand. Your views will represent you, and must be presented in a manner that shows you have the best interests of the company, not just your department, at heart. Your views count—make them known.

# 5
# EXCESSIVE PAPERWORK

*Excessive paperwork* is another area of concern, not only in the office, but at home as well. One look at your desk at home can tell you if you keep too many papers. Do you need all those papers? How often do you weed out the unneeded papers? Look at your pocketbook. How about your wallet? Do you find yourself carrying too many papers? By weeding out the excessive papers, you will save time when you need to find one of the important papers.

Yes, you can do something about excessive paperwork. There is an excellent story about the two construction workers who made it a point to eat lunch together each day. Both men brought their lunch from home. They would discuss the contents of the meal. Joe had a different sandwich each day. Fred, on the other hand, had the same lunch each day, a turkey loaf sandwich. One day Fred looked really sad while eating his lunch, and Joe asked, "Say, Fred, why don't you ask for a different sandwich; you would enjoy your lunch more." Fred turned and said, "I don't think that would work. I make the sandwiches myself!" This story is characteristic of the numerous people who complain about excessive paperwork but never do anything to help solve the problem. The statistics on the cost of paperwork, and the numerous hours spent on this task, are not as important as the loss in morale of your workers doing this excessive, often boring, paperwork. You must decide how much of this paperwork you should do.

A manager in Vermont wanted to cut the paperwork and increase the operation of his company. In order to do this he displayed a large sign over his desk at his office: DO IT RIGHT THE FIRST TIME. This statement is as relevant to the janitor, mailboy, secretary, or junior manager as it is to the company president. Doing it right the first time might very well mean getting a machine like a computer or word-processing machine to help you. By watching your paperwork costs you will also be watching your expenses. Each dollar you save the company will be one dollar more on your profit-and-loss statement of the company. Time is money.

A large retailing company found that in a three-year period with the introduction of eleven word-processing systems with numerous video-display work stations dispersed throughout the country, they saved more than $900,000. The company wanted to give their stores the top service in order to increase profits. Their systems are located in the merchandise, corporate personnel, auditing, credit, not-for-resale purchasing, controller, and legal departments of the company.

The word-processing machines cut duplication and saved many dollars. They produced a huge amount of printed literature from personnel manuals to store procedure manuals. It was a multiple-step project. First, type up the work, send it out to the printer to be typeset, and then have the work printed. The solution to this costly procedure was to purchase a machine to make the job easier and cheaper. The company purchased an in-house phototypesetter so that extra typing would not be required. This change cut excessive costs and thereby increased profits for the company. For example, using the old method, sending the work to an outside typesetter cost $25 to $40 per page. With an in-house phototypesetter, they can do it at a mere $5 per page. With thousands of pages to print, the company saved both time and money.

One personnel director in Florida, Charlotte S., tries to keep her own paperwork at a minimum by setting aside two hours a month for discarding paperwork no longer needed. Charlotte finds that many departments seek her advice to cut down on excessive paperwork. She likes to send both the manager or supervisor of the department, along with an employee like a clerk (someone that is familiar with day-to-day paperwork problems) to a seminar dealing with this topic. She believes in dealing with paperwork problems on the lowest levels, and that by going directly to the people doing the paperwork on a daily basis, a faster, easier solution can be found.

Let's say that for every dollar you earn in sales, you make a profit of 4 per cent. If you can save $16,000 for your company by cutting down excessive paperwork, it is equivalent to a $400,000 sales increase. The additional value of cutting down on excessive paperwork is that you will have the time to do your "higher payoff" items. Never permit fear to get into your avenue of success. Fear is the greatest enemy of success in cutting paperwork down—fear that you may offend the people that set up paperwork in the first place or fear that your ideas will never work. Your new idea might be new and unique for doing something faster, better, more easily, or more economically than it has ever been done in the past.

Do you write numerous business letters? The latest cost estimate for an average business letter is now close to $10 per letter. Perhaps you can buy a form letter book giving you the best letters possible for your routine letters. One manager is reviewing letters by his employees to determine if these letters are necessary. He also recommends that they make an effort to answer a letter by simply writing out the answer by hand, right on the original letter. The basic rule to save you time is to handle each sheet of paper only once. If you decide to keep the sheet of paper on your desk, it may become part of the larger pile of other sheets you have kept for the last few months. If you feel that you know the information well, or someone else in your department or company will have this information on file if you need it in the future, toss the sheet of paper in your wastebasket. Get a larger wastebasket if you need one. Get your name taken off the distribution list of the memorandums that lack real relevance and meaning to you or your department. Communicate your feelings about paperwork control to your supervisors or managers and those working under them for the maximum results.

How are your competitors or other companies handling their paperwork challenges? During a seminar on management, one executive talked about the use of new multipurpose forms to cut paperwork cost. This idea was used in one company so that one form could be used for both the purchase requisitions, purchase orders, and invoices. Other companies can give you information on the latest machines such as the word computers or home computers that can help you accomplish your goals. Try to make your work easier and simpler so that you can have some extra time.

Do you spend too much time filing your papers? Filing costs are very high and increasing each year. Too much sand passes through the hour glass because people want to save a copy of the letter, the graph, the report, or the sales projection. How many people are filing a copy of the report? If three or four departments are filing a copy of the report, this is a good example of duplication of filing. Why not have one department handle the filing for specific reports? Do you review your filing procedures periodically to determine the possibility of duplicate filing? Do you hire capable people to handle your filing? One manager found that by hiring a well-trained person to do the filing, much time and effort was saved from trying to find misfiled papers and reports. Try to limit access to the files in your office to certain people who will be responsible for your filing system. Do your part to help the filing situation in your organization by discarding non-essential papers. The experiences in most firms show that over one-third of all material received in a normal work day should be thrown away. The best way to avoid excessive filing is to dispose of the non-essential papers first.

You may also find new ways to add hours to the daily work days for other workers or associates in your office. You may find that some workers have information on various scraps of paper and other information on wall calendars, while other information is kept in their shirt pockets or personal wallets. These haphazard systems require that many minutes and hours of each day be spent trying to find the data, or trying to determine where the data were originally stored. Why not combine all of these tools into one? One time-management system that keeps all your information in one book. The book can include a to-do list, appointments, things to remember, and even a section that includes things to do the next day. A very aware time manager and owner of a small business knew that his father, also an employee of the business, was scattering his energies, thereby diluting his efficiency. He scattered his notes and information all over the office. Since the father's job was scheduling trucks transporting goods all over New England, it was important that some new tools be used to add hours to his day. The son recommended that the father use one book to organize all the data so that time could be better utilized. Initially the father rebelled because it was a new idea and he wanted to continue using the old, tired methods of the past. The son convinced him to try the new method. The father tried the new method and gradually it worked into a far better time management system. Once the system went into operation and produced success, everyone was happy. The son was happy because he no longer had to worry about one or more of the scraps of paper becoming lost. The father was happy because he had learned a more efficient way to use his time. It started with a better idea.

One of the real problems behind excessive paperwork is the paperwork expert—the individual who is willing to take on extra paperwork assignments without finding out how important the paperwork happens to be or trying to find an easier way. One company dealing with government contracts had thousands of employees. In their large clerical department, a gentleman by the name of Fred Jones had a clean desk. He always seemed very organized, to the point that he was always looking for work to do. B. Smith, another worker in the same office, was just the opposite. His in-box was filled with work, his desk had piles of papers, and he was always running out of time. One day they met in the company cafeteria for lunch and B. Smith asked a question he had wanted to ask for months. "Say, Fred, how do you manage to stay so organized? Your desk is so clean and you're always ahead of your work!" To this Fred Jones replied, "Well, since this is such a large company, when I get some paperwork or work I really do not want to handle, I simply write SMITH on the top of the paper and put it into the intercompany mail. In a large company like this, we're bound to have someone named SMITH."

# 6
# POOR
# COMMUNICATION

Good communication can help you in your battle against the clock. Many problems, mistakes, misunderstandings, and failures result from the lack of communication or *poor communication*. A participant in a time management seminar wants to talk to her boss about the reasons why he takes on so much extra work. She is reluctant to talk to him because, in her words, "He just wouldn't understand." A very popular writer finds that his time is being consumed by numerous unplanned visitors at his home. He would like to spend his time doing other things. He now feels he is a prisoner in his own house. In order to get out of this dilemma, he must communicate his feelings to these people making the unannounced visits. You must try to build successful communication networks at home, at work, in your private life, with the people you like, and with the people you dislike. Here are some examples of communication failures:

- "But dear, you told me to make the reservations for Friday. I didn't know you had other plans."
- "Sorry, but I was not informed that the meeting was cancelled until Friday."
- "I was never told that my customer was unhappy with his purchase."

- "I left the note on his desk—I didn't know he was out of town for the week."
- "I know the report is due every month. No one told me to send it to the main headquarters."
- "I was sure that the contract would be signed on Friday."
- "I was under the impression that three flights left Houston each day. I didn't know they had reduced it to only one."

Try not to take for granted that other people know as much as you about your specialty. Work hard to reach an equal understanding. Take the necessary time to communicate clearly and completely in order to avoid repeating the instructions or correcting mistakes in the future. The normal reaction is to blame others for any communication errors. You must play your part to communicate well. It requires an all-out effort by everyone in your office from the clerks to the president of the company. It means taking the time to listen, and besides listening closely, looking the other person directly in the eye. It means caring to take the time to explain a point or a concept so that the other person can benefit from your knowledge and experience.

Many companies are starting communication programs. A large telephone parts company is presently spending thousands of dollars and many man hours to put together a communications program for their supervisors. The company did some extensive research on their communication networks with their employees and found the best time to build good communication networks is when the supervisor evaluates the employee yearly for a salary review. The company requires all supervisors to attend a day-long seminar to fully understand the technique in the salary review communication process. The yearly salary review is a very special time in a person's life, and once the review is over the worker will continually think about what was said during this salary review. Most workers want to do a good job, and for doing this good job they want to be paid a good wage. A good supervisor rewards the good worker with the raise that is justified, and the worker that has room for improvement must be told about his poor performance in a diplomatic manner by the supervisor. People are very sensitive but they also want to know how the employer feels about their work.

How do you communicate your unhappiness? One manager of administration in a national electronic company is a master in motivating and communicating to his people. Here is how he communicates to one of his people during a salary review:

"Jack, you get along with others in the office very well. You get your routine jobs out on time and from all reports your work is average. But Jack, I feel that you are not working quite up to your potential. I feel that you should be coming up with more creative ideas on how you can run your department and your people even better than at present."

Now that he has communicated his unhappiness, his next step is to listen closely to the response from Jack. Listening is extremely important in the communication process and there are four basic steps in this process. The most important one is simply to hear out the individual doing the talking and learn what his or her reaction is. Listening skills are difficult to train because many people start thinking about what they want to say next and never take the time to hear the individual speaker. Take the time to give your full concentration to the speaker. It's very difficult to listen to a speaker at home when your favorite television show is on. One gentleman discovered that his mother-in-law was coming to live with him. He asked his wife about this, and she replied, "I told you about it during the football game that was on last Monday evening." No wonder he didn't remember it. He admitted that when the football game is on, he never hears anything else. While the television is on very little listening can be accomplished. Take the time and make the effort for full listening.

The second step in the listening process is to interpret what is being said. What does your wife mean by that statement? What does your son mean by his conversation? What does your husband mean? If you have a problem interpreting what the person is really saying, you can ask him to repeat part or all of the statement. Some excellent listeners save time by summarizing with such statements as:

- "Jack, what you're saying is that you feel the five-year plan can be completed by next December, if you get the help?"
- "Anne, your mother will come to live with us only if we can add another room to our house, is that correct?"
- "Greg, you only made three wrong answers on the test. Why do you still feel you need extra help?"
- "I realize that your performance is good in our marketing department. I still cannot understand why you want to switch fields."
- "I know you have a great deal of work, but why not delegate some of this work to others in your office?"

Interpreting what is said is difficult. But without carefully hearing what is said, you will never be able to fully interpret correctly. Not only must you interpret what is being said, you must also respond to the speaker, and what has been said, or permit the speaker to continue. Here are some examples of responses:

- "Yes, that sounds very important, go on."
- "Betty, I don't understand what you mean by that last statement. Go over it again in layman's terms."
- "If you feel you were treated unfairly by the supervisor, please give me your reasons."
- "You cited four possible reasons for the strike. Do you feel we can work each one out?"

Listening is essential in all areas of your life, but it takes a tremendous amount of effort on your part to develop this skill. Just as the athlete must keep him- or herself in shape in order to compete, you must keep your listening skills in the same top shape. One family in Oregon found that the television in their house was robbing them of a very important game called conversation. In order to play this game they decided to restrict the amount of television viewing. Although each one in the family had the right to choose his program, all of them decided to make a real reduction in their viewing time. What other time-robbers do you have at home and in the office standing in your way of proper communication?

Take the necessary time to ask the right questions. A bank manager asking the right question on a loan or financial problem can make the difference between success or failure. The right question or questions will help you avoid the extra call back on the telephone to get the answer later. When I have an appointment with a doctor, I try to have a list of questions that I will ask the doctor when I see him. The cost is the same for the appointment whether I ask one question or six questions. An insurance agent asking the right questions can develop a creative insurance program that is tailored to the needs of the business or individual. A manager who asks the right questions can save his company both time and money.

Good communication is good time management because people want you to take the necessary time to make them feel comfortable around you. You might feel that you're making great gains in your management of time, and accomplishing great goals, but unless other people like you and feel that you're interested in them, you will have a difficult time reaching your goals. A recent study of high school students found that over 80 percent of the students questioned felt that their guidance counselors lacked the necessary time to devote to their career guidance needs. One student felt that when a guidance counselor has five hundred students assigned to him, it leaves little time for individual counseling. Just as the individual worker looks forward to the salary review, the individual student looks forward to career advice to mesh with his or her educational experiences in high school.

Good letter writing is a very valuable skill. A well-written letter shows people that you can express your ideas in a logical manner. A good letter will help you sell you and your ideas. Take the time to carefully plan what you want to say in the letter. Take out any extra words so you give a clear message. Once the letter is sent out, keep a carbon copy of the letter on file. You will need this copy to ensure that some type of positive action is taken on your letter subject. One time manager in a paper company puts a carbon copy of the letter in the "tickler file" so that he can check if an answer is received by a particular date. In many cases the difference between a good communicator and an average communicator is the latter's lack of persistence in following up on important letter subjects. What letters are really "high payoff" communication items? You might consider letting your secretary write and sign your routine letters. The more important letters are signed and checked before being sent out. Good time management is getting complicated matters on paper. Why make an oral agreement with someone on a complicated matter? Wait until you have a chance to think it over and get the information into writing, so that you and the other party can agree to it and sign it. Too many oral agreements get clouded, diluted, and mistaken with time.

Communicate with your boss. You must be a good communicator to sell your ideas to your boss. During a recent time management seminar one of the attendees asked, "Just what do you do when you have a boss that needs time management?" If your boss is wasting too much of your time and you cannot get to see him or her, you must communicate your unhappiness to your boss. Try to build up a good communication network with your boss. Let's look at some of the ways you can do this.

Develop a relationship with your boss that will grow and endure. What does your boss like to do? Is he or she interested in sports? What school did your boss attend? Where does the boss live? What are the main things you have in common? Did you ever share a funny story with the boss? What happened at work or at the golf course that you can share? Your value to your boss will increase when you assume responsibilities. Each boss has strengths and weaknesses. Boss "A" may be excellent in technical knowledge, but poor in people problems. If you help the boss in handling the people problems, you will aid the boss and the organization.

Understand your boss. He or she may be involved in thinking about the whole organization. You may restrict your thinking to just your department, job, or office, but your boss is concerned with the climate of the whole organization. Changes within your office or your company will affect the way the boss reacts to you and everyone in the office. Read your boss's feelings and get to know how he or she reacts to different situations. You will be able to make the relationship work if you make an effort toward building a relationship that will survive with the passage of time. Once the relationship is developed, you can then work toward your goal of getting more work from your boss.

Communicate with your secretary. You can save a lot of time and trouble if you make an attempt to communicate fully with your secretary or assistant. Your secretary should know where you are at all times and how you can be reached. Keep your secretary informed as to when you will be back in the office. When you're traveling your callers will want to know how they can reach you. Your secretary should be aware of your priorities so that she can work with you successfully to meet your objectives.

Also important is communication at home. One of the best ways to improve communication on the home front is to take the time to ask questions. One of our neighbors decided to move to another town. Since their ten-year-old son delivers the paper, I asked him why they decided to move. He said there were a number of reasons, but the important one was a misunderstanding. "My mother moved into the house because she felt my Dad liked it. My father moved into the house because he was sure that she liked it. As it turns out, neither one wanted to live there." Make sure that you understand each other and do not take your ideas or assumptions for granted.

*Good communication saves time and money.* Do you take the necessary time to communicate completely with your employees and associates? Many times managers find that by concentrating fully on face-to-face communications with their subordinates, time and efficiency is increased within the organization. One manager from Maine found himself communicating face-to-face with only some of his workers, leaving the others in his office feeling at a definite disadvantage because of not "hearing it right from the boss." This can cause a morale problem.

I had the experience of seeing a business lose money because of a lack of communication. A head secretary wrote a memorandum describing the new purchasing plan for air travel tickets. By use of a certain air travel vendor, a substantial amount of money could be saved by the firm. Another secretary, who is very bright and capable, ordered single tickets for her boss, instead of using the special vendor who offered a much better price. If she had taken the necessary time to talk to the head secretary about the new procedure, the loss could have been avoided. No company can afford to be without proper communication. Proper communication can save time and money. It must exist at all levels of the organization.

# 7
# SOCIALIZING

Socializing is another timewaster. How much time in every office and the working world is spent visiting and talking about the personal interests? Small talk can be a real time waster and keep you from getting to your number one priority. Not only will the small talk waste your own time, but also the time of any other people in the office willing to listen to it. One secretary in a large service company spent over two hours on the phone setting up her cocktail party for Saturday evening. Joe, in the machine shop, extended the coffee break by over fifteen minutes talking about how the Super Bowl football game should be played.

Socializing is usually the end result of a normal business conversation; once the conversation is completed for the business items, the social conversation starts. One housewife from Massachusetts discovered, by running a check on her time, that she spent a large part of her day chatting with her friends across the street. Another large chunk of time was spent on the telephone. She found that it was very difficult for her to explain to her friends that she had other things to do at the time. She decided she wanted to start an exercise program at a local exercise salon. In order to do this, she would need some of the time she usually spent with her coffee-chat friends and her telephone friends. She didn't cut the full time from her friends right away, but each day she cut down on this time so she could use the time on her new priority. One way she found to make it easier to cut down on her socializing time was to think about the good results she would attain from the exercise classes. She thought about the ways she would look in a bathing suit, and how she could wear her new summer and fall outfits.

Fred C. found that his in-box was always full of work, but when he looked out the door of his office his workers were spending a good part of the day socializing with each other or on the phone with personal calls. After doing some checking for a few days he determined that the reason for the socializing was that too little work flowed out of his office to the other workers. This situation gave Fred good reasons to delegate more of his routine work, work that could be started by others or work that needed some initial information before it could be moved ahead. Fred decided to delegate more of his work and noticed that the socializing decreased at the same time.

Socializing is a normal time waster in every company. People work because they want to socialize and meet other people. We are social animals. People want to be with other people. A certain amount of socializing is normal. Excessive socializing by certain employees can damage a company or organization, and you must make an attempt to find out the reason why this excessive socializing is taking place before you can do anything about it. Why does Sue spend so much time talking to Betty in the general accounting office? Why does Harry carry on so long about his boating and water sports? You might want to speak to the people about this situation and get their side of the story. I worked in one office where a woman spent a great deal of time socializing because her boss refused to give her enough work to do. You must also watch your own amount of socializing—it might be an attempt to avoid starting on your top priority for the day.

# 8
# SETTING PROPER
# PRIORITIES

The first internal time waster is the *lack of proper priorities*. This subject was covered earlier in the book, but the top time managers always find ways to get back to the top priorities. Putting down your priorities on your to-do list is only part of the answer. You must be willing to stay with your top priority for a sufficient amount of time to accomplish it. One way to prepare yourself to set priorities is to get yourself ready to accomplish your objectives. One of my students, Michelle B., went back to college last fall after being out for over fifteen years. She took basic liberal arts subjects and tutored music as a part-time position. She wanted to make a move in her career into the business field and major in accounting. By taking a few subjects in the accounting field, she would get enough information to help her make the final decision about the field.

Michelle B. received excellent grades in these college accounting subjects. Her grades and self-confidence grew to a point whereby she decided to start a masters program specializing in accounting. She likes to tell me that I had something to do with building her confidence by telling her "You can do it." But she also had the right background, the right level of maturity, and the right desire to reach her priorities. She set her priorities into proper order and reached her goals.

Your priorities must also take into account your own satisfactions. What makes you happy? Would you be much happier as a teacher than as a principal? Would you feel more at ease as an administrative assistant rather than as a supervisor? Setting priorities that will give you satisfaction are very important to you. According to Gallup's 1980 National Survey on Families, 33 percent of women feel that the ideal life for them would be to be married, have children, and also hold down a full-time job. This new trend is causing many women to set priorities that will be very difficult to attain. To successfully complete them involves getting cooperation from many other people. It means that the husband and wife must work together to help reach their priorities. One large corporation hired two women to work in the sales department for a large division. The women went through the sales training program and were doing an excellent job in this department. The job required some extensive traveling and the women knew this when they accepted the position. Three months after they started the job, they both left the company. They left the company not because they failed in their jobs, but because their families had a difficult time adjusting to their new roles. Their husbands could not handle the excessive traveling by their wives, and therefore the women had to quit their careers—at least temporarily—in order to save their marriages. This situation might have been avoided if the women had taken the time to appraise the required action before taking the positions. Can you hire someone to care for the children? Can an agreement be made between you and your husband to make the career change work for you? Can you switch some of the OUR work to your husband? Your mother? Your mother-in-law? Your other relatives? Your childcare personnel? A combination of all of the above? Your priorities can be accomplished when you give sufficient time to appraise the required action. The above story of the two women that took sales positions only to quit later represents a feeling that 'women must still take the main role in rearing the children, and keeping the family together, even when they accept full-time positions.' Although this view is changing, women must consider this view in their planning to reach their priorities.

Your clearly defined priority will enable you to plan each day. Let's say, for example, your goal is to become the manager of your department. Each day at work you will set daily goals to help you get the experience you need to qualify for this position. Without this priority you might set daily goals that are just average goals and not ones that offer the experience you need to move up in your job. As you accomplish the daily goals, you develop the confidence to take on larger and even more important goals.

I have a son who was a very slow learner when it came to learning how to swim. I tried to motivate him by stressing the benefits of learning to swim. Nothing worked. He refused to give it the necessary effort and energy to succeed. I received a poster showing two pictures—one of a small boy frightened stiff about jumping into the pool, and the second depicting the boy in the water doing all kinds of swimming strokes, enjoying the water and his new-found confidence. The caption on the poster said:

"Every accomplishment—great or small—starts with the same decision: I'll try."

I hung the poster up in my office at home. My son came into the office and read the poster. I talked about it with him. Soon afterwards he passed his swimming class with flying colors. He now is eager to swim every chance he has. He has tremendous confidence in his swimming abilities. To reach your priorities make the best effort possible. You can attain the results you seek.

Take a look at the priority form below, and list your priorities, in no special order. Just make a list of them. You may want to learn to play golf. You may want to spend more time meeting new friends. You may want to start your own business. You may want to stop smoking. You may want to spend more time reading your latest batch of books. You may want to join the local PTA. You might want to gain experience in a particular field so you can make a career switch. You may want to volunteer some time to a local organization. Just make a list of your priorities in Illustration 5.

Now what is the most important priority to you? What priority is the highest priority in terms of "high payoff" to you? Why is the

| DATE | PRIORITY |
|------|----------|
|      |          |

**ILLUSTRATION 5.**

priority a special one to you? Is it the highest priority to you? Now in Illustration 6 list your priorities in terms of their importance to you.

Now that you have listed your priorities in the order of importance to you, try to put them into your to-do list every day. Try to start one each week. Try one every Monday evening. If you want to learn to paint, sign up for that class at the local high school or college. If you want to learn to dance, sign up for the class starting this coming Thursday evening. Too many people have priorities but never take the time to do something about making their priorities come alive. The only way your priorities will come alive is when you make them a part of your normal time. Once the priority gets on your to-do list, you're well on your way to completing it.

| DATE | NUMBER | PRIORITY | REQUIRED ACTION |
|------|--------|----------|-----------------|
|      |        |          |                 |

**ILLUSTRATION 6.**

*Use your "tickler file" to help you accomplish your priorities.* Just what is a "tickler file" and how can it help you? A tickler file is just that: a file or a notice to tickle you to accomplish a particular job or assignment. Rick H., a successful advertising executive, has developed an excellent method of using the tickler file: he assigns the secretary the job of keeping the tickler file filled with dates, names, and projects he would like to accomplish. Each day his secretary will go to the tickler file to determine what items are set aside for Rick to accomplish on this particular day. One day it might be simply to call a potential customer to set up an appointment for a sales presentation. Another day it might be a reminder to accomplish a certain job for a present customer. The tickler file might have items a week old or items as old as eleven or twelve months.

This same "tickler file" technique can be used at home as well. Instead of writing down the items to do in a separate file, you can ask your children, husband, or wife to help you remember to do a particular task. Recently we went to a graduation exercise and a party following the ceremony. Since we didn't have the necessary time before the ceremony, I asked my children and my wife to remind me to purchase some spring water and drop off some books at the library on the way back from the party. As we reached the vicinity of the store, my daughter shouted, "We must pick up some spring water . . ." It was my tickler not only to accomplish this job, but also to drop the books off at the library just up the street. The tickler file may sound like additional work for you, but if you take the necessary time to develop it you may find that it will work to save tremendous time and work for you.

*Do you spend too much time trying to find the most important work?* In a recent time management seminar, a few people found it difficult to determine the most important work. They questioned whether they should work on job A or job B. The ideal situation is one in which you can spot the highest priority quickly and easily. Don't spend too much time trying to do this and never expect your boss to determine this for you. You must go to work without delay on what you feel is the most important priority in your job. Bob H. is a printing salesman and he made it a point to call on one new account each morning to increase his sales. He found that setting a priority in his list of items to do each day gave him the opportunity to reach this goal. He found the sales increasing because he sold some of the new accounts. Successful time managers find that including the "must do's" in their list of items to do each day helps them reach new horizons. As long as you're working on items you feel are important to you and your job, you will finish those difficult-to-accomplish jobs. As one secretary in a large Boston firm commented on her accomplishments for her company, "I just stay on the 'must do's' until all are completed. In the past I just put them off, but now I just stay with them until the end. The system is working. I will stay right with it now." Planning your work is fine, but try not to over-plan, and tackle the items you want to accomplish.

*Do you find yourself doing the jobs you like at the expense of the more critical jobs?* One manager found that he was spending a large amount of his time looking at the financial aspects of his job. He knew that his previous jobs and educational training were in this area. He made the decision to take the necessary time to look at the whole job rather than the portion of the job he felt was important to him. What takes the largest portion of your time? Do you enjoy doing the routine work? Do you enjoy working on certain problems because you personally find them interesting? Do you find yourself more efficient with particular kinds of work? One way to solve the problem of spending large blocks of time on certain jobs is to ask yourself this important question: "Is this job essential to the final accomplishments of my goals within the organization?" When you can answer this question with a yes, then take the necessary time to accomplish this job.

Press on to reach your "high payoff" jobs. One very successful mother, wife, school teacher, and local politician was asked why she was so successful in juggling all of her obligations so successfully. She replied, "I make a careful list of each item I want to accomplish during the day, and I assign a letter to each one. The very important items are given the letter *A*, the important items are given letter *B*, and the routine or lower items are given the letter *C*. I go immediately to work on the A items, and I move from the last A item to the B's. I try to get some of my students to help me with the C's. I feel that by giving my students this work I will help them grow. I also have a small sign on my typewriter to remind me to delegate some of the typing to the secretaries available to me. I just keep trying to do the most important items first." This is an excellent example of why many people give the extra work to the busy people—simply because the busy people find new ways to get the work done on time.

Calvin Coolidge was known during his administration as the "silent" president. He made this important point:

### PRESS ON

Nothing in the world can take the place of persistence. Talent will not; nothing is more common than unsuccessful men with talent. Genius will not; unrewarded genius is almost a proverb. Education will not; the world is full of educated derelicts. Persistence and determination alone are omnipotent.

— Calvin Coolidge

Add hours to your day by going right to work on the essential work. Do the important work rather than avoid it. The people who accomplish important work do so because instead of finding excuses for avoiding it, they face the work head on and complete it. You can avoid the important or hard-to-start jobs by doing a variety of smaller, less-important jobs. For example, let's say you have a five-year plan to complete for your boss. This five-year plan details what the company plans to do in sales and production in the future. To avoid doing the plan you could spend time doing the research instead of the actual writing of the plan. You could spend time doing smaller unrelated jobs that have no relationship to the five-year plan just to pass some time. You could talk to other people within your office or associates about the plan and how the results of the plan will be used. You could spend your time procrastinating about the job or finding numerous reasons for delaying the plan. All of these examples indicate ways to avoid doing what you know you should be doing in the first place. Instead of spending the time and energy avoiding the important work, get started on it. Visualize yourself doing and completing the job. Visualize yourself getting a reward from your boss, such as a large raise or promotion because of your performance. Only you can face the important work and get busy on it. You may find that once the important work is started you will enjoy it and feel better. Once you complete the difficult-to-start job, you can then give yourself the reward you deserve.

# 9
# AVOIDING PRIORITIES: PROCRASTINATION AND HOW TO BEAT IT

"When I get more time I will finish the playroom." "When I get more time I will write that novel." "I want to do it, but I cannot afford to spend the time right now." All of these statements have some validity and truth to them, but they are also methods we use to avoid plunging into our number one priority. In many cases you delay working on your number one priority by procrastinating, hoping secretly that it will go away by itself. The number one priority will not go away, and you may find that delaying it longer and longer makes it even more difficult to start.

For example, I know one very successful businessman, Bob V., who built his publishing and printing business over a period of years. He started the business in 1963 and the first year's sales were only $6,300. He was determined to build the business, he didn't let procrastination defeat him, and he just kept expanding the business by hiring more help and increasing the sales of the business. Bob V. doubled the sales to increase the business to nearly $250,000 in sales fourteen years later. At that point the business required more professional management in order to make it succeed. Bob V. decided that rather than spend the time in managing the business, he would try to start additional products and businesses. In starting these new products and businesses he really was procrastinating to avoid doing the essential work of proper day-to-day management of his first business. Bob V. was an idea man, a person who was well-read and always looking for new money-making ideas. Yet these ideas became time wasters to him and his business. The procrastination process absorbed valuable time each day, and left no time to do the management that was so important for the business. The end result of this situation was a bankrupt company. Now Bob V. still has those numerous ideas to work with, but he's without the regular capital from the business to help support the ideas.

Another young lady, Maryrose G., has a nice career in nursing, with advance degrees in the field. She has an idea to make certain products to help in the nursing field. Some of her ideas are good ones, but she keeps procrastinating about her business ideas and products. In order to start this new business she must develop a plan of action. She enjoys talking about the business to her friends and relatives, but the process goes little beyond the talking stage. Her plan of action could be to write a description of the business, and the products and services she plans to sell. Once the description of the business is complete, the next step would be to make a full description of the market area. Which consumers will buy the nursing products? How large is the group? Is the group large enough to support the business? Once she knows her market, the next step would be to study the competition. What companies will compete against Maryrose and her products? Will the consumers buy her product before considering the competitor's? The final step in the plan should be to describe the talents, abilities, and educational backgrounds of the management of the company. Will they lend specific expertise to help the company succeed? Then, armed with these plans, she could move into the operation of the business.

Maryrose G. is not unique. Thousands of small business people this year will open various businesses, and at the start of their businesses most are very confident they will reach their goals for success. The statistics tell another story. Out of every one hundred businesses started this year, only twenty will survive five years. One in nine will last beyond seven years. Only a small percentage of the small businesspeople take the necessary time to write out their business plans. One businessman said he carried the plan in his head. By avoiding the formal writing of your plan, it's easy to waste time and procrastinate.

"*I know the job is important and I will get to it as soon as possible.*" It's easy to put off jobs we care little about, and easy to work on other jobs we enjoy. Habits are difficult to break, but you can change your habits and your work style to accomplish your "difficult to get to" jobs. In high school Charles B. always delayed doing his homework and studying for tests until the last day or the last hour before a critical test day. This habit gave him a reputation as a procrastinator and pulled his grades down. After completing high school he entered the service for three years. He went to work after the service and then started college in the evenings. He determined that during his new start in college he would stay ahead of his work and do each assignment as soon as the assignment was given. It worked for him. His grades were better and he developed an important ingredient in successful time use: the fine tuning of his self-confidence. He felt great about himself and his ability to accomplish school work by putting in the adequate amount of time.

Charles B. was amazed; he had abilities and talents that were starting to bloom all over. He amazed his family, his buddies, and his working associates. The evening school courses developed "key potentials" that opened up new opportunities for him. He enrolled in college during the day for a degree in business. The school started on a Friday and that day an assignment was given that was to be passed in on Monday. Charles wanted to go out Friday night, but now he was faced with an important goal. Since he wanted to stay clear of the procrastination problems of the past, he stayed home to complete the assignment. This was a very important and valuable example of discipline that was characteristic of the remainder of the college experience: finish the work correctly and on time. Charles is a different person now because he took it upon himself to choose his allotment of time. He avoided the problems of the past by doing the important work right away.

I have a seminar entitled "The Ten Best Home Businesses," and a description of a business plan is fully described on the opening evening of the seminar. I find that only a handful of the students will take the seminar and their time seriously enough to include the business plan in their future plans. Some people delay the business plan because they feel that the plan must be perfect to do the job. Why feel you have to be a perfectionist? You are not a professional business consultant, so why do you expect to do a perfect job on the plan? Just do the best job possible. Once you develop the plan you will have a direction-setter, something to use as a guide to help you reach your goals. The first step is always the most difficult in any project. Once started, many things will happen; you will, one hopes, receive some positive feedback that will help you to move on with the job.

One such example of positive feedback happened to Alex Haley, author of *Roots*. Many years before he wrote the famous book, Haley was busy writing short stories and articles and sending them out to various publishers and editors. Each day he received rejection note after rejection note. He claimed he wanted to paper his writing room with the various rejection notes. Most of the notes started with "Sorry, this does not meet our needs at this time." Finally, he received a rejection notice with a small handwritten note, "Sorry, this is a nice try. Keep trying." He was elated. No sale to the editor, but now this gave him the psychological reinforcement to keep trying. The editors were not really computers and machines after all. One editor took the time to write a small note to him. This gave him the motivation to continue to write. He now felt he could make it. If he had given in to the common problem of procrastination he might never have received this very much needed motivation to move ahead in his writing career. Haley admits there are many better writers around to top his best work, but some of them may have procrastinated long enough in their writing to delay and finally impede their success. If you give in to the temptation of procrastination often enough it will become a lifestyle and you will never get on with your number one priority.

The procrastinator and the pessimist are partners and they support each other in their avoidance of the number one priorities. The procrastinator seeks objects and things to keep him or her away from the "high payoff" work. He will be happy to stop at the desk of the pessimist, or even call the pessimist on the phone to share their common interests. The pessimist will be happy to consume and steal some of your valuable time for you. He or she will shoot holes in every idea, plan, goal you can offer. This is very comforting to the procrastinator, because the procrastinator didn't want to do the job anyway. Let's listen to the conversation:

Procrastinator: "Say, I'm thinking about starting a new advertising campaign for the company, especially for our newest product."

Pessimist: "Don't tell me anything about our advertising program. I never liked the ads. The competition's ads are so much better. It's a waste of time and money."

Procrastinator: "We need a new campaign. I think your view is common of others in the company."

Pessimist: "Sure, this company is not moving in the right direction. I have said this right along. Our company cannot beat the competition."

Procrastinator: "I really didn't want to do the new advertising campaign anyway. Your views make me feel even stronger about dropping the whole idea."

Pessimist: "I'm always happy to help you. Keep me in mind with future projects or ideas."

Notice how the pessimist spread gloom on the idea for the advertising program? The pessimist can waste his own time stressing negative points on your idea or project, or that of anyone who is foolish enough to listen to him. It's always easier for the pessimist to shoot down things, but you will never find him giving specifics of why something is wrong, or how it can be fixed. It's one thing to talk about the negative aspects of a subject, still another to be sympathetic to the current situation. Why are the ads so poor? Why is the competition so much better? Why is the company managing itself this particular way? The pessimist has many questions about why something is done in a particular manner, but no answers or positive contributions to aid in the solution. The best way to avoid the pessimist is to make a detour around his or her desk. If he stops by to talk to you at your desk, make the conversation as short as possible. Manage your time effectively. If you're presently in MY time, and you're avoiding a number one priority, take every precaution to avoid the pessimist. If you run into him at this time you will not only lose valuable time, but, just as the conversation with the procrastinator showed, you may come to fully believe you cannot do the project.

Another way to avoid the number one priority is to listen to the "soft information" at work or at home. Soft information is the information available to you in the form of gossip and rumors of the department or company. How do you respond to this information? Some otherwise successful time managers are excellent workers on their number one job, or "high payoff" jobs, but take too much time to listen to the rumors and gossip. One very successful time manager summed up his method of avoiding spending his time on idle gossip this way: "I have all I can do keeping up with my own work, let alone trying to investigate and handle other problems." The procrastinator is easy prey for the gossip and rumor mills. He wants to spend his time on anything but the job he's trying to avoid at the time.

My roommate in college would spend a good part of the day and evening socializing and gossiping with his friends. At the end of the evening he would then come into the room to do his work. It was not unusual for him to start his work around midnight and work until morning. He could have used his time and energy more effectively by trying to get as much work done as possible during the earlier hours and going to sleep earlier in the evening. The system this gentleman used never worked for him, and before long he had left the college for other pursuits.

Another very important time absorber for the procrastinator is the television set. A recent study shows that 87 percent of all households watch television during their leisure time. Almost seventy million households watch television on a regular basis. The biggest problem with television is that the programs are set up so that you will sit down to watch programs for three or four hours at a time. You may only want to watch a certain program but discover other shows around that program designed to get you to watch a full evening of television. Can you restrict your television viewing to only certain hours, or certain days of the week? Run a check on how many hours you use your television set. Can you use some of this time more effectively? Do you use the television set as a procrastination aid? One of my close friends got into a habit of watching the afternoon shows on television. Even when she was busy with a top-priority project, she would delay it to watch the shows. She was hooked on the shows and wanted to see each one. Since the shows are on in the afternoon, when the energy level of most people is high, it tended to break up her whole day—and make it very difficult for her to get back to her other priorities. She had a problem that is common to many other people. She wanted to do the "high payoff" work and enjoy herself as well. She took some quiet time of her own and found an answer to her time-management dilemma: why not tape the programs in the afternoon while she was doing her higher-priority work—writing her short stories—and play the tapes later in the day when she had the time? There is an answer to everything if you give yourself enough time and effort. Without the natural answer to this problem, she would have felt a little guilty about watching the programs and not doing her work. Now, by taping the shows, she can watch them once or twice a week depending on her time and schedule. Now she is in charge of the television programs; the programs are not directing her. She is now managing her time, and not vice versa. Think about your own interests and conflicts in your time management. You might be able to use this idea or a similar idea to help you get the best of both worlds.

Many people procrastinate because of fear. What do you have to fear? All of us have some fears. It's common to be afraid of the unknowns in our lives. If we continue to think about all the different fears we have, or all the bad things that could possibly happen, we will further deepen our fears. Psychologists claim that only a very small percentage of the things we fear ever happen at all. One of the best methods to cut your fears to a minimum is to focus on your current goals. How are you doing on your current goals? How did you start on that goal? Can you use the same method to develop a new goal? What is your lifetime goal? Do you want to be the very best computer specialist in the country? Do you want to be a manager in your company? Do you want to be a college instructor? Do you want to get married? Do you want to make a date with a particular person? Do you want to go on a famous television show? Do you want to go back to school for another field of study? Do you want to start your own business? Do you want to learn to swim? Do you want to be a better public speaker? Do you want to spend more time with your children or your grandchildren? Do you want more time to be alone? One of the best ways to beat your fears is to prevent your fears from taking too much of your time to grow. Successful time managers minimize the amount of time they give to their fears. They would rather spend that time and energy on their current projects. Your current projects become important parts of your total time-management plan. The puzzle will come together successfully when you spend your time on the current goals, even when the goals are not perfect.

Procrastination is fueled by people afraid to make mistakes. Are you afraid to make some mistakes? Just like Alex Haley, who wrote a number of books and stories before he finally attained the great success of *Roots*, you must continue to try and try again in order to reach your goals. Your mistakes, big and small, will aid you in developing confidence for the future. All successful people become successful by making mistakes and then profiting from their mistakes, and doing the job a little better the next time. Procrastinators will tell you that the project is not quite done because there are a few minor details to complete before it's ready to go. These minor details are never completed, or are delayed to the final deadline. The procrastinator never has to worry about failure because the work or project will never be evaluated since it's still on his or her desk. The job is still just work in progress, not finished work. The work is not completed because the procrastinator wants an "A" for his work and will not settle for a lower grade. To some people, grades are more important than content.

The first day of class for my Accounting I students at a local college was spent discussing the overview of the class, the requirements for the course, the grading system, the type of tests, and other relevant information about the course. I also stressed the benefits of taking a course in accounting and how it would aid in the career opportunities for the students. At the end of the class, a woman about forty came up to my desk to ask a question about the course. I was happy to reiterate the benefits of the course and how it would be an aid in career or job development. She said to me, "I'm on a particular program and I have received straight A's in all my work. I want to be certain that these marks will continue for me." I congratulated her on her success, but told her the following: "I cannot guarantee you the same high grades, but I will guarantee that you will learn the principles of accounting from my course." The lady thanked me very much for my time. She left the course that day and never returned to my class again. This is a good example of a person with confused priorities. The content of the class was secondary to the top grades.

A college student who tried very hard in his English Composition class received a grade of "C." He asked the instructor about the grade and the response was that the standards of the course were very strict, and his work was only worth a "C" from the instructor. The student was mad because he knew he deserved much better than the grade he received. He finished college and started writing for various magazines all over the country. He had an article published, and then more and more. He wanted to send some of the articles to his former college instructor, partly for spite, and partly for his own ego. The instructor was very happy to see one of her students reach such success in the writing world. Her comment to the former student was, "This is excellent. I have never had another student receive such success in their writing. I'm very proud of you." In school, as in life, never let the grades you receive, whether on your report card or on the job, stop you from reaching out for higher-priority work and doing the work better and better each time. Perfection in your work is important, but not as important as your persistence in getting the important work out each day.

One example of this is a college instructor who manages his time to accomplish many different jobs. In a recent interview Professor J. admitted that for many years he had been a die-hard procrastinator. Then one day he had decided to try more things in his life, and with a new confidence in himself, he had taken on other goals and objectives. "Time won't wait for you," says Professor J. "It's like a circus—always packing up and moving away. A procrastinator thinks time will be there later." And now a procrastinator Professor J. is not. He is a teacher at two colleges, an author, lecturer, accountant, consultant, entrepreneur, and family man. He is primarily a "night person." His normal working day begins at eight o'clock and doesn't end until midnight, when he unwinds with magazines and television late news. Fortunately, he can function properly with six hours of rest. Professor J. claims the guilt wheel spins when he begins to procrastinate on important jobs. He'd rather work smarter, not necessarily harder. He feels programmed to a certain degree, but programmed to do the specific things that make him happy.

Another example of a former procrastinator is Richard F., a full-time police officer in Massachusetts. He watched with pride a number of his children carry degrees off the graduation stands at various colleges. He wanted to go back to college to prove to himself and his family that he could do the college work as well. He had some real fears about whether or not he could accomplish the work. In the past he had claimed he could not go back to school because he was putting his children through school and could not take the time. Now that most of his children were grown up and on their own, Richard F. was put on the spot to move on his tendencies to procrastinate. He decided to take some action on his goal of going back to school. He signed up for a course at the local university. At fifty-two, this father of nine children took his first class in law enforcement. He was successful in the first course, so he signed up for more. This technique is very important in conquering the procrastination problem. Take at least one step to complete a goal you want to accomplish. Richard F. developed so much confidence in himself after the success of the first course that he then devoted more time to the studies, and completed the normal four-year program in a year and a half. His grades were excellent: all A's except for two B's. He did this by applying himself to the goal for the full year and a half. He slept only about four hours each night. He readily admits that he did not reach this achievement alone, but with the help of his family, his wife, and the university. In your goals you must realize that you alone can accomplish only so much and you must be able to get other people at work or at home to help you. Richard F. knew he could not back down from this goal. He told his children he could do it, and this worked like magic to force him to do it. The best ingredient to beat procrastination is make the job or your goal a challenge to you. Prove to yourself you can do the job. Once you accomplish the job the next most important step is to reward yourself for it.

# 10
# DELEGATE
# TO LESSEN YOUR LOAD

*Too little delegation* can be a great time-waster. At a recent meeting of our church committee, the chairperson, Bill V., presented a new assignment for the next month—the budget for the next fiscal year was now due. Bill has shown a real ability to handle the chairperson's job, and one of the reasons for his success is his ability to present the assignments and projects, and then delegate the work to committee members ready and willing to do the work. Once Bill took the time to explain what and how the budget work could be completed, and showed he would be willing to lend some of his help to complete the work, four members volunteered for the job.

Do you really believe that the people in your office can do the job? Gene S., an office worker in an electronics company in New Hampshire, found that although he had three people working for him, he took on many of their jobs. When he was asked about his taking on this extra work all by himself, he claimed that his employees could not handle the work correctly. Gene S. lacked confidence in the other workers in his office. This lack of confidence forced him to spend time on numerous OUR time activities, which eventually would seriously cut his MY time. Permit your workers to grow on the job. Let them develop their confidence by doing their own work and you can work on even higher-priority items.

*Build the skills in your organization to help you save your valuable time.* You can only do a certain amount of work yourself. You are fighting both the clock on the wall and your energy resources. One of the ways to help you win the battle with the clock is to get others within your organization to help you accomplish your organization's goals. The more work you can share with your employees the more energy you will have in reserve to tackle the important and long-range issues of your choice. You have the choice of doing many of the routine jobs or carefully assigning them to others. In order to assign jobs to others, you must make certain they have the skills and training to do the jobs correctly. For example, when I worked in an office as the office manager, I knew that one of the women in the office was going out on vacation for a week. I made the comment, "Joanne, I hope you have a nice vacation next week." She replied, "Thanks, but I will not go on vacation until Tuesday; I must come in on Monday to prepare the payroll. I'm the only one in the office who can prepare the payroll." As the office manager, I didn't want to be put into the position of being forced to rely on one person to do the payroll. I immediately trained another worker within the office to handle the payroll so that everyone could take their vacations when assigned. I was no longer forced to rely on only one person to do a particular job. I make other employees in the office grow by learning new jobs. Do you "grow" people in your job?

One successful time manager in California found he could beat the time wasters by concentrating on getting more work done through the efforts of other people in the office. He spent one complete morning fully analyzing the skills and talents of each worker in his department. Along with this inventory of skills and talents he also considered other important information about the people. Bill Smith in the clerical department worked well under time pressure. If the job had a deadline for the end of the month, Bill had the ability to produce on time. Betty Arnold, on the other hand, found time pressures and deadlines made her too nervous and slowed down her ability to perform certain jobs. A good manager must use daily working experience to fully determine which individual responds to tight work schedules and which one cannot handle it. Knowing your personnel can help them use their time effectively. Do you know and use your people?

*Get to know the people within your organization to help you manage your time.* Who is the most important person in your department? Why is that person important to you? Do you rely too much on this person? Do you find yourself spending too much time trying to please or maintain your relationship with a particular person or group? I worked in one company primarily engaged in the production of paper. One of the favorite departments was the maintenance shop. It became a favorite because the workers there had a different project each day. One day they would be fixing a trailer, the next day they would rebuild a diesel motor, or another day it would be the rebuilding of the rear-end of a tractor. A number of people within the organization spent a good deal of their time going to this department, much to the neglect of their own departments.

One very successful manager in Massachusetts finds that by making regular tours of the plant he gets a feel for the plant as well as getting to know his people even better. He would arrive at the company in the morning and instead of coming in the front door, he would come in by the back door and greet the numerous production workers. He found that by using this approach he could develop a better relationship with his workers. This has helped to communicate a very important concept: You are an important part of this company, we need you.

A supervisor in Maine found that when he successfully delegated some of his work to others in his company, he rewarded himself by giving himself a longer lunch hour alone. He found this lunch to be vital for gathering valuable ideas to help him do his job better. This time alone gave him the time to plan for upcoming jobs at his company. He also used the time to store away some mental energy to tackle future jobs. This valuable time alone gave him added determination to succeed.

What is the best time of day to delegate work assignments? This question is an important one. No one wants to receive a job, whether large or small, late in the day. One study on office productivity showed that many people reach their peak of efficiency during the late morning hours, around 11:00 A.M. to 11:30 A.M. The peak will last for about one hour and then taper off the rest of the day. Try to get the work to other workers in the morning so they can work on the job during the peak energy period of the day. Remember that proper time management means monitoring closely your own energy level as well. You have only so much energy each day and you should use it on the most important work. If you delegate work assignments to your employees early in the day, your chance of getting this work finished is much greater than if you assign the work later in the day.

What do you do when you have a series of delegation problems in your company? You will never be able to assign work to your supervisor or assistant if they in turn fail to delegate some of their work in order to prepare for you. Take the case of Vicki H., a manager of public relations in Washington, D.C. She found herself with too much work, and each attempt to delegate this work was thwarted by her subordinates' claiming they had too much work already, so that she could not get to her own additional work. Vicki reached the end of her patience and called her top assistant, Tom C., into her office. She asked him to give her a list of the various jobs he was presently doing. He listed about five different jobs. Vicki wrote each job down on a sheet of paper. By further analyzing these jobs together, both Vicki and Tom agreed that of the five jobs, two jobs could be handled by the secretary in their office and another job could be handled by another department, so only two jobs out of the five required Tom's attention. Once the three jobs were sent to the right people and departments, Tom was ready to accept some of the work from his boss. In order to successfully delegate, you must make certain that your assistants are minding their own time correctly. Vicki noticed that this series of delegation is a problem not only in her own office, but in the company as a whole. Too many bosses and managers just assume that the workers are doing work that is top priority and never take the necessary time to check it out.

Many teachers in both the private and the public sectors spend many hours preparing materials to use in their presentations in order to keep up a high level of instruction in their classrooms. Some teachers are so efficient they take on typing assignments that could be done by the typing pool at the school. Teachers have to protect their time so they can be as creative as possible in the classroom. Why not delegate this typing and other nonteaching jobs to people who are assigned to do this work? One teacher of history found that a number of jobs could be delegated to his students. Many of his students were eager to take on jobs to help lessen the teacher's load, and permit the teacher to do what he is paid to do: teach his students.

Do you use your secretary in your delegation program? Many time managers use their secretaries to handle the routine secretarial duties such as screening telephone calls, typing letters, handling routine mail, handling the "tickler file" (covered earlier in book), and many others. How many other jobs can you delegate to your secretary? Do you fully utilize your secretary? Do you set up a particular time each day to discuss the activities of the day? Sometimes if you discuss some of your pressing problems with your secretary, she will be able to offer advice or assistance on working out these problems. Nothing makes a secretary angrier than not being part of the team. Never take your secretary's talents and abilities for granted.

Do you find your desk piled high with work? Do you delegate enough of your work? Do you feel that you are the only person in your office who can handle your work? One manager in Louisiana found that his workload continued to increase to the point where he asked his boss to hire another assistant to help lessen the workload. The request was turned down. The manager made a complete survey of all the work he handled each week and each month. He found that too much of the work was of a routine nature and he felt that this work could be handled by a machine. He made another request to his boss for the purchase of a mini-computer to handle the routine jobs. The cost was only half the cost of hiring a full-time assistant and it was a one-time cost, unlike the salary for an employee. The request was granted. The manager purchased the mini-computer and now finds much more time to do what he was hired to do—to manage his department. There is a very common element in this story that is important in successful time management and that is the ability and persistence to sell your ideas to help you in the battle against the hour glass. Notice how the manager first asked for the assistant. Although refused, he went back to the drawing board, found routine work was involved, and then made the request for the mini-computer, which was approved. Selling, selling, selling your ideas can make the difference between wading in work up to your hips, or being able to do your job your way. Sell the most important product: You.

The statement so common in numerous offices all over the working world is: "I'm tired. I know I'm doing too much work myself." Why not investigate more opportunities to delegate some of that work? Can you hire someone to handle some of the work for you? If so, you can delegate some of the work to the recently hired employee. How valuable is your time? One manager tried to determine the value of his time and much to his surprise found his time worth well over $100 per hour to his company. If you are worth over $100 per hour, it is worth your while to delegate the routine work to other people.

Make sure that you know the work you want to delegate. Good delegators are people who are familiar with the work they want to delegate, and who have the ability to explain the important points in the jobs. It is not necessary to explain every detail, but you should be able to make the job sound interesting and important to the company. The expert delegator will say, "Say, Betty, we have a real problem with the invoice to the ABC Company. Please check it out and send them a corrected bill. This is an important account and we want to make sure of our billing to them." Notice that the delegator didn't simply hand the job over to Betty. He explained the problem and the reason for the job being assigned to her. Good delegators can even make you feel that because of your special skills, talents, or abilities, you can do the job better than anyone else in the company.

Use the same time each day to assign or delegate your jobs.

For instance, Mark V., a senior accountant for a governmental agency in Washington, D.C., delegates his routine jobs around 11:00 A.M. each morning. He calls one person at a time into his office and delegates the work. This has become a work style for him. His workers now look forward to that time in the day when they will talk to Mark and take some work with them.

Delegation may require both persistence and motivation. The ability to delegate is a skill that takes time and effort to perfect. In my experience working as a manager, I enjoyed seeing the executive getting it all together and delegating, controlling, and relating to others in the office. Many managers find that to delegate successfully they must have confidence in themselves and the work they control. Once you have this feeling of confidence your people will work harder for you. They want to feel they work for a successful person; people want to associate with success. In a recent college class, I had one young lady say to me, "Mr. Bond, you really believe in us— you really believe we can learn this difficult subject." I responded by saying, "Yes, I believe in you, and I believe in myself." Be persistent and believe that you can accomplish your goals.

Jimmy M., a sales manager in Ohio, found that once he delegated numerous jobs and assignments to his salespeople, the work was never completed on time and in the manner he wanted it done. In following up on these jobs with his salespeople he found that he received numerous excuses for the failure to complete these jobs. After keeping a log of the various jobs and salespeople, he found that the biggest offenders were the salespeople who lacked confidence in themselves. They seemed to have the confidence to do the daily calls, but on new calls their lack of confidence slowed them down. Jim did two things when he delegated to these salespeople: he told them about their benefits and assets, and reminded them of the importance of the job; and he made certain that when the job was completed successfully, he took the necessary time to thank them. Jim is blessed with a very positive mental attitude. He tries to pass on that mental attitude by encouraging his workers with trust, praise, and compliments. Jim has a large poster on the wall in his office that successfully delivers an important message:

When faced with a mountain I will not quit! I will keep on striving until I climb over, find a pass through, tunnel underneath—or simply stay and turn the mountain into a gold mine, with God's help!

Every job must be handled with care but the most important point in good delegating is to resist the temptation to expect perfection in the jobs. You might very well be able to complete the jobs better yourself, but that will never help people grow within your department. Managers that expect extreme levels of perfection from their employees develop nervous assistants who feel they shouldn't bother to do the job since the boss will never be satisfied.

Save time by giving proper instructions. Charlie S. is the manager of an art studio employing ten commercial artists, and in order to make a profit in his business he must get his money's worth from the artists. Although he tries to assign work to the artists based on their individual specialities, some assignments are so different and unique that it is difficult to find the proper match of artist and assignment. Charlie S. does his best to find out what the artist knows about the job. If he finds that the artist knows the job, Charlie delegates it to that artist. On the other hand, if the artist is unfamiliar with the job, Charlie will teach him or her the basic elements about the job. He even makes illustrations and graphs to fully instruct and answer all pertinent questions. Once the assignment is discussed, some basic teaching completed, and all questions answered, the assignment is given to the artist to complete. Charlie makes certain to avoid overprotecting the artist. He wants to be certain that he gives the artist the time and necessary room to do the work.

Watch closely for reverse delegation. Many managers assign tasks but are willing to take them back just as soon as the employee has a problem. How can you relieve yourself of routine jobs if you take the task back so soon? You will develop a reputation as a poor delegator. How can you get promoted to the next job in your company if you're so important doing all the little, medium, and large jobs in your department? Why not ask the employee to work on this task a little more? Answer any questions the worker might have, but make him or her do the work. Let's take the example of Karen P., an assistant personnel manager. Karen delegated to Larry T. the preparation of a rough draft of a new policy on sick leave for the company. They discussed the subject completely, Karen answered all questions posed by Larry, and the job was started. After working on the job for one and a half days, Larry wanted to get help on the project, and he asked to speak to Karen about it. Here is the conversation:

Larry: "Karen, I ran into a problem with the sick-leave policy project."

Karen: "What is it?"

Larry: "I cannot determine just how many days are fair and equitable for our sick leave policy."

Karen: "What are the other companies in our industry doing in this area? How do we compare with others?"

Larry: "I didn't get into that information yet. I know I need more research information."

Karen: "Complete research is essential for policy determinations. Although our company library is limited, you might want to visit the Kirstein Business Branch of the Boston Public Library. They have the latest periodicals available there."

Larry: "I never gave the library a thought. I will go over there tomorrow. Thanks."

Notice what happened here. Larry started the task but he wanted to unload it on Karen after working on it a very short time. This is common practice for certain people, to quit as soon as a few problems start to pop up on the horizon. Karen in this case refused to take the task back. She presented the idea of the library as a research source to keep the task on the right track. Once Larry discovered how he could get more information, he could move ahead on the job and add to his confidence for future jobs.

A good delegator can recommend the best source of information. How many projects or tasks are never completed because of the lack of information? How much work on projects is a waste of valuable time because of the lack of necessary information? One very important source of information is your public library. The reference librarian of your public library is also available to you for your questions. If your public library cannot give you a book you need, request the use of the inter-library loan program. This special program will send your request to the numerous libraries in your area and within a few days you will receive the book you requested. Many cities also have specialized libraries to help with various jobs. In Boston, the Kirstein Public Library serves the business community by offering industrial, commercial, and professional directories for the United States; industrial and commercial directories for foreign countries; investment services and manuals; books and pamphlets on business subjects; periodicals pertaining to finance and trade; and numerous government reports and annuals. This fine business library offers three floors of information specially geared to the business person. Do you make use of these valuable sources of information?

In order to delegate to selected employees successfully, you must have a working knowledge about the specific talents each person working with you possesses, and also what skills they need to acquire to become more important in your company. (In order to be successful in delegating the right tasks to the right people you must try to assign the same tasks on a regular basis.) Some delegators make the mistake of changing the tasks and people on a steady basis and in doing so prevent growth in the staff and in the overall organization. The chart below will help you to keep track of the delegated tasks.

| Assigned Date | Task or Job Assigned | Comp. Date | To Whom | Remarks |
|---|---|---|---|---|
| 4/17 | Rough draft of policy on sick leave. | 4/30 | Larry T. | Excellent job. |
| 4/17 | List of injured employees last year. | 4/21 | Rhonda C. | Fine job. |
| 4/18 | Research on fringe benefits plan. | 5/15 | Albert T. | Fair/Needed Rewriting. |
| 4/19 | Cost/Benefit Analysis on job enrichment.. | 5/21 | Fran V. | Good. |

**ILLUSTRATION 7. DELEGATION RECORD**

Delegation success will help you not only if your boss leaves for another job or is promoted, but also in performance evaluation. Performance evaluation is when you periodically discuss and evaluate an employee's performance on his job for the last six months or for one year. The more delegating you do, the more knowledge you gain about the strengths and weaknesses of the employees in your department. How can you do a better job on the performance evaluation? This evaluation can be a real motivator for the individual employee. You may very well determine employees with potential for promotion. You might also inform the employee how he or she has performed during the last twelve months. A great deal of research in employee motivation shows that this performance evaluation is the single most important meeting for your employee during the whole year. You can give out the rewards by patting him or her on the back if the performance deems it, and you can also point out the areas of possible improvement. People want to feel that their work is acceptable and that their contributions are helping to build a sense of security within the organization. A favorable performance evaluation or one that tends to focus on their strengths will help build the sense of achievement so necessary for the confidence for future development.

One manager in a large electronics company, Ronald G., has a special performance evaluation technique that works very well with his employees. Let's move into his office when he gives part of the performance evaluation to a personnel supervisor, Jason F.:

Ronald G.: "Jason, I'm very happy with your ability to move out much of the routine work. You also did an excellent job on the manpower planning analysis for next year. I'm more than a little concerned, though, about your ability to perform when the job requires extensive interaction with other supervisors and your employees."

Jason F.: "Thank you very much for the kind words about the manpower planning analysis. I worked very hard on that project. I know I work harder when I'm working on a project by myself because it's easier to control the quality of the work.

I'm also happy to hear that you realize I'm doing a number of reports each week and month for the company."

Ronald: "Yes, but quite frankly Jason, I hired you to supervise your department. Since you have three employees in your department, you should try to delegate more of your routine work. This will lighten up your load so I can give you some special projects we promised the main office."

Jason: "Yes, boss, I want to start some of those special projects, but the workload is still very heavy, especially during this, our busy season."

Ronald: "Since you're a supervisor, Jason, I want you to make an effort to delegate more of your routine jobs to others. If you set a goal to delegate two jobs each day to each worker, that's six jobs a day, and thirty jobs in the course of a week. Once you set up a system like this, it will become a work style, and your workers will look forward to the extra work."

Jason: "That idea sounds good. I'll try it immediately."

Ronald: "I will note this on the performance evaluation, and if the next evaluation shows you are meeting these delegation goals so that you can accomplish the special projects, I would say your next step up would be to assistant manager."

Jason: "Fine. That's just what I wanted to accomplish during this performance evaluation. I want to be the next assistant manager."

Notice how Ronald G. used the "strength building" technique to zero in on a few of Jason's weaker areas. Once the weaker areas become evident, solutions can be found. The solution in this case was for Jason to delegate and relate better to other people within the organization. Ronald G. helped Jason decide on a mutually agreeable goal for the next performance evaluation—the goal to delegate more to accomplish the other work so important to both parties. Ronald G. wanted the special projects completed to lessen his own load, and Jason wanted to do them for the experience, but to find the time to do them required delegation to his own workers. The reward for the successful completion of these goals was the assistant manager's job.

The value of rewards is enormous. Once you delegate the work, make certain that you take the necessary time to reward the individual for this "better work." A large advertising agency held monthly meetings to which all employees were invited, and the executive manager would make a statement to the whole company about the "better work" by certain employees. Other companies reward by writing memorandums to the specific employees and other members of their department. In order for rewards to be effective, they should be given as closely to the time the exceptional work was performed as possible. Some companies give special "employee of the month" awards to reward excellent work. Many successful time managers find that waiting for the performance evaluation takes too long and makes the reward ineffective.

Take the example of Emery Air Freight Company. A few years ago they found that excessive profits were being lost because many packages were being packed in boxes too large, thereby using too much space on the planes. Quite simply, the employees didn't want to take the necessary time to do the job correctly. They just wanted to do the job quickly with very little concern for quality control. The company considered a number of options to solve this problem, such as a new training program, a large deck for packages, hiring more people, a supervisor's training program, and many, many other costly ideas. The company finally decided on a program that was very inexpensive, but it had two parts: a feedback program, whereby the employees measured their work to a particular standard; and a reward when they reached a particular level of performance. The supervisor or manager thanked the individual for his or her "better work." The reward in many cases was no more than a pat on the back, or a statement as simple as "very, very good, keep up this excellent work." The cost of the program was a few hundred dollars to print up the performance forms, and several thousand dollars for executives to monitor the performance of the program in the various plants all over the country. The final savings will be well over $400,000 for the company. But the real benefit of the program is not just the dollars, but the intangible benefits of making the employees feel they are a valuable part of the team. This program was just as important for the women that worked on the telephone sales as the men that worked as truck drivers picking up the packages at the customer offices. They became motivated to beat their records for the previous day. They wanted to make a contribution to the company. This involvement with the mainstream of the company helped some of the employees to suggest ideas about how the company could improve their operations even more. One truck driver mentioned to his boss a new way to save time (and thereby money) by taking a certain highway during an especially busy time. He mentioned this new idea because of the new rapport that developed between the workers and the supervisors and management. Now the people worked as a team and not just as employees for the company. They now felt their efforts were appreciated and respected by management.

## Summary

Delegation is an essential part of proper time management. Without proper delegation you will find yourself doing routine jobs. You will find yourself taking on too many jobs and running out of time. Delegation can also be beneficial when you find that your workers are caught up in their work and in need of more challenging assignments or projects. Parents can get excellent experience in delegating tasks by carefully delegating to their children many of the daily chores at home. Delegating is not an easy job, but with practice and persistence it will give you the time you need to accomplish jobs and assignments to reach your own goals.

Good delegators are excellent listeners, but discipline themselves from taking back the work from the delegatees. Good delegators can hint and constructively suggest and recommend new ways to help complete the job. A good delegator knows that delegating in a systematic and creative manner will help other people to grow under his or her direction. A good delegator knows the enormous importance of rewards. People want praise and recognition for their good work and you must make people feel good about themselves and their abilities.

# 11
# DON'T SPREAD
# YOURSELF THIN

*Are you spreading yourself too thin?* Too many people that complain about their lack of time and their work overload are guilty of trying to take too much control within their organizations. When you "spread yourself too thin" you're going to pick up much of the work that was originally issued to your subordinates. An article in the *Harvard Business Review* vividly described a manager trying to solve all of his subordinates' problems (commonly called "monkeys"). At the end of each workday he had five to seven monkeys on his back. One Saturday morning the manager was working very hard to handle his many problems when he looked out the window of his office only to see the seven subordinates spending their Saturday enjoying their golfing. In order to keep his health and his sanity, the manager decided to take the monkeys off his back and place them where they belonged—on the backs of his subordinates.[1]

Just as this manager found himself taking on too many monkeys, he reached the point where he could not care for and feed the monkeys any longer. If the monkey is not needed, why should you look after it? It consumes a great deal of your time to care for and feed these monkeys. Why not shoot (eliminate) the monkeys you don't need? Well, if you feel it would be unfair to

1. William Oncken, Jr. and Donald L. Wass, *Harvard Business Review*, November/December 1974, p. 77.

shoot the monkeys, why not take the necessary time to give the monkeys back to their originators? Let Ted handle the monkey himself. After all, he knows more about that monkey than you do. You could do the research and make the proper decision, but didn't you hire him to do supervision work to make some decisions? Take each monkey off your back and put it where it belongs or shoot it. You cannot complete the work you're hired to do if you try to take on too many monkeys yourself. You are better off helping other people to grow and protecting your most precious resource—TIME.

By spreading yourself too thin you can expect one of the following things to happen: you will be so tired by trying to do the impossible that your work will be at best only mediocre; or you will find that trying to keep up that impossible pace will expose you to the possibility of physical breakdown which could be fatal. I worked for a president of a company, Henry F., who spread himself too thin. He not only wanted to be involved in every one of the day-to-day company problems, but he was also extremely involved in many other activities outside the office. His excessive workload and overstrenuous schedule resulted in a very serious heart attack. Henry F. was an intense guy. He loved to compete, loved to win, enjoyed his business, his friends, his employees, and life. He was a person unable to say "No" because he wanted people to like him. He liked people and he had a real need to have other people like him also. How many things can you accomplish during your MY time? What about your OUR time? Your BOSS time? Surely you want to accomplish as much as possible, but you also must be realistic about when too much is too much. Henry F. would call me at all hours of the night to check some business facts concerning a business meeting the next day. One time he called about an accident that happened in the plant during the night. Henry always had his hand on the pulse of the business and he was also always willing to go to great lengths to help a friend or even a friend of a friend in many situations. Henry F. should look carefully at the priorities listed in Illustrations 2 and 4, and then determine to handle only the priorities that have the highest payoff for him. You cannot put all available jobs, tasks, and requests on your to-do list unless you want to care and feed a tremendous amount of monkeys, and at the same time weaken your sanity and your health. One gentleman leaving a time management seminar remarked, "I must go back to my office to look after my monkeys. I hope now I can get rid of some of them." The best way to avoid too many monkeys is to be aware that you're receiving them. You will continue to receive them unless you're able to protect yourself against them.

Trying to be a "super worker" can hurt your time management. During a recent time management seminar I had one manager indicate several times that he was frightened that he could not please his boss. Many people in the world of work spend a great deal of time and energy worrying about their boss asking for information they don't have or a question they cannot answer. You're only human; you cannot expect yourself to know everything. Even a computer can only answer a certain number of questions. In order to answer other questions, the computer will require a new program.

One college professor sums up this very important problem of wanting to have all the answers. When asked about the reason for requesting a leave of absence, he replied, "I'm not a reservoir of knowledge. It's time to replenish the source." Your boss or supervisor also knows this. When you're asked a question which you cannot answer, simply say, "I'm not sure of the answer to your question. I will take the time to find the answer for you."

I found that many recent college graduates in new jobs try too hard and find themselves worrying about pleasing their bosses instead of simply doing the best job they can do. The boss knows you cannot know everything and in most cases he or she will think more of you if you admit you don't know the answer but are willing to do the necessary research to find it. One very popular talk-show host in Boston is a specialist in many areas, but the one area he knows nothing about is local sports. When he gets a question on this he simply tells the caller he knows nothing about sports, and he is respected because of his honesty.

Take the case of Henry F., a bright, energetic business executive who took his business over from his father. The business was never truly turned over to Henry because he was continually trying to please his father in every decision and action he took for the firm. Why not try to please yourself? Do you feel good about yourself? Why try to please others continually and accept this real time waster for you? In the case of Henry F., he was not only concerned about pleasing his dad, but many others as well. He was going much too fast, trying to accomplish too much and please too many people, and the end result was a massive heart attack. Trying to please others is simply impossible; you will please some people, but others will never be satisfied. Satisfy the most important person: YOU.

We live in the age of specialization, and when the manager tries to look after monkeys of many different species, shapes, and sizes, a tremendous amount of problems can occur. In the medical field for example, it's very difficult to find a general practitioner. With the specialist, he or she can take the time to really study and understand every situation for that particular field of medicine. In engineering, accounting, dentistry, administration, food service, retailing, publishing, and many other fields there are specialists to save time and better serve others. Do you specialize in certain areas so you can offer better service? Or do you try to be the "jack of all trades" and handle many wide-ranging subjects and problems? In short, do your own thing but be careful of the problem of taking on too many monkeys. This quote sums up my feelings:

"No one can succeed at everything—but everyone can succeed at something."

                                                              Anonymous

# 12
# CONFIDENCE

The lack of an "I can do it" attitude can be another important time waster. In my time-management research project, I found a common characteristic of good time managers: each one possesses an attitude of "I can do it" and "I want to give it a good try." This attitude was developed after a number of successful accomplishments in their organizations. The only way to keep a constant positive attitude is to be willing to give yourself the necessary credit for your accomplishments of the past and your abilities. Your mood can influence all the people around you. If you show self-assurance and a real feeling of confidence, this attitude will create a chain reaction in all the people around you. It will help you in dealing with others in your department because people like to be around people with a positive "can do it" attitude. In order to accomplish that difficult job you must feel that you can do it. One woman I know wants to open a small shop in a nearby town to display her numerous paintings. Each time I speak with her, she tells me about this idea. The cost is not too high and the job is possible, but she must make the decision to do it. In order to make the final decision, she must believe that she can do it. She must develop an attitude of "I know I can do it" and "I'm going to try it." She is very confident in her work. She can talk and explain the style, technique, and philosophy of her artwork, but she finds it difficult to project a positive attitude about how she can reach her success. Although she has won numerous awards for her work, she still feels that since it is not selling for large sums of money she is not a complete success. Why not focus on your strengths, your assets, and your special talents and not on your shortcomings? Why not focus on success? Believe in that special person you see in the mirror each day. You are special. You are unique. There will never be another person just like you. Never sell yourself short. Believe in yourself. You may fall down a few times trying to reach your goals, but so what? You will be a better person for it. All successful people reach success after dealing with many failures along the way. You can turn failures into successes, but you must believe in a very important person to do it: YOU.

Another friend of mine, Albert V., is the owner of a florist business. He wants to computerize the operation of the business to help save time and money for the company. Albert V. feels that too much time is being consumed by routine paperwork handled by hand. Computerizing the business is a very important priority for Albert. But each time he presents the problem to his partner, he finds his partner putting the idea down, telling Albert all the problems with setting up the computer such as costs, time to install, teaching others to use the computer, etc. This excellent idea originally developed by Albert will never see the light of day because Albert cannot develop the "I can do it" attitude to make it work. How many people do you know who would like to write a book if they could find the time? How many people want to go back to college to finish up for that degree, but keep putting it off? If you believe that you can do it, you're well on your way to reaching your goal, whatever it happens to be.

Another hazard that will slow your success involves the numerous people that spin the guilt wheel on you, trying to erode your confidence. The only way to handle people who do this to you is simply to turn the wheel in their direction. For example, a woman who graduated from a popular art school at the age of fifty wanted to pursue a lifelong ambition—oil and water painting. She invited her mother to the graduating ceremony and during dinner after the impressive ceremony, her mother asked, "Mary, just what do you expect to do with this education at your age?" Mary was taken aback by this remark, but was quick to reply, "I plan on doing what I do best, painting the best oil and water paintings I can do."

Bill V., a young business executive, was telling an associate about his ideas, plans, and objectives for building his company into a leader of the business opportunities field. The associate replied, "Bill, if you're so smart, why aren't you rich?" Bill was surprised to hear such a remark from the associate, but he replied, "Just what makes you so sure that I'm not rich? I'm rich because I have ideas, goals, and also use my time in the best manner possible." This left the associate with very little to say except, "Oh, yes, I never looked at it in that manner before, Bill." If and when the guilt wheel moves in your direction, simply stop it and spin it back in the direction of the original wheel spinner.

Parents can play an important role in helping their children feel confident about themselves. I tell my children that they are special, because they possess special talents unique to them, and that they should make every opportunity to utilize their full potential. Last winter my daughter sent some of her artwork to the local paper to be considered for their contest of "What Christmas Means to Me." Each day the paper would include the artwork and the names of the winners. My daughter would look over the artwork and the names of the winners, eagerly looking for her work and her name to appear. It did not appear. She was discouraged, and said to me, "Dad, I feel my work is better than the people that are winning." I replied, "Why not call them to tell them how you feel?" The upshot was that we called the paper to explain her feelings, and they told us that the competition was intense, and that hundreds, perhaps thousands, of applicants had applied to this contest. My daughter lost the contest, but she became a winner because she believed in her work. She felt that it should be declared a winner. In order to win the battle against the clock, or the battle for the promotion, or the battle for the most sales, or the battle for any contest, you must believe that you can do it.

Don't be fooled by looking at other people. Many people size others up by saying, "He's so confident. I only wish I had his talents and abilities. He seems to have an immunity to any fear or worries." These same people that have the look of confidence are filled with many of the same fears that you have, but they continue to overcome their fears by concentrating on thinking about their abilities, and how they can accomplish certain jobs and assignments. All of us have a certain number of fears. Many people fear failure, and never try some difficult projects because they feel they cannot win.

The most important knowledge is knowing yourself—knowing all of your strengths and weaknesses, especially the former. In your job you will be dealing with producing either a product or a service, but you must realize immediately that in your personal career YOU are the product. The product is you. Know the product. Improve the product. Know both the advantages and the disadvantages so you will be able to sell yourself at a higher market value. A successful advertising manager once remarked, "Every product has a place in the sun." As an aware businessperson, you must also look for your place in the sun.

It is a very difficult job to get to know the type of person you really are—not just the type of person you think you are. An excellent way to find out who you are is to write a self-appraisal that identifies your major personality traits. Take sufficient time and be as honest as possible with yourself. No one knows your personality better than you.

Do you really know yourself? Do you know your real self? Never mind the way your parents see you. Never mind how your children see you. How do you see yourself? What do you enjoy doing? What activity do you enjoy more than any other? Why do you feel confident doing this activity? Do you enjoy working with machines? Or working with your hands? Or working with numbers? Or with people? It's difficult to answer these questions off the top of your head. To answer these questions you must analyze all the things that make you *you*. You will benefit if you write out a self-appraisal. A self-appraisal can be developed after fully exploring your knowledge of yourself. Here is an example of a self-appraisal:

My assets include a good basic intelligence, good personal appearance, a liking and understanding for people, a good sense of time, and an awareness of the importance of planning. I enjoy competition and sports. Politics and the study of successful people are among my chief interests. I enjoy starting new projects and once a project or program is completed I move on to another. I strive for balance in my life. For example, I allow so much time for enjoying my family, so much time for meeting with my friends, so much time for reading, so much time for studying, and so much time for my job.

I have an excellent memory, especially for names and faces of people I have met and associated with in some manner. I remembered almost every class member at the tenth class reunion.

Working as a paper boy in junior high school, I enjoyed meeting new people on the paper route. Vocational counseling at the Veteran's Administration showed that my strong interests were in the business and social science areas.

An example of my ability to work with people is my experience in attaining my part-time job in the Army. I worked the switchboard while I was stationed in New York, and this job gave me the opportunity to learn the names and locations of a variety of officers within the post. One day when a Major in charge of the Officers' Club made a long distance call, I asked him whether there was any part-time work available at the club. He told me to check with a sergeant at the club, who in turn said he needed a dishwasher. A few short weeks later I had an excellent paying part-time job as a drink waiter in the main dining room. I not only worked well with people, but I also took risks to attain my goals.

On my first job after college, my boss told me my best asset was my ability to work with people. I have an ability to get people to talk about themselves because I listen attentively to what they have to say and I remember a good deal of what they communicate to me. During my three years in the Army, I recall giving some of my buddies a good deal of my time, just listening to their problems and ideas.

Communication has also been one of my key points. One of my first college courses was Effective Public Speaking. I contend that this course was one that gave me the confidence to meet people, ask for jobs, and even ask for a college scholarship. I accidentally stumbled onto one of my key potentials, a potential that once introduced helped me to direct myself. I went on to become a teacher, win a scholarship, and earn a master's degree as well as a wife.

My assets continually point in the direction of my ability to work well with people and to my ability to communicate.

When you do your self-analysis take sufficient time to determine trends in your personality and your outstanding assets. Getting to know yourself can be a very rewarding experience. Once you know yourself and your skills and assets you will be in a better position to use them. It is also important to know your shortcomings so that you can propose a program to improve on them.

You should attempt to make your strong points pay off for you and to overcome your weaknesses. If one of your weaknesses is the lack of confidence in speaking in front of a group, try to make a pertinent contribution during your next meeting. An evening speaking course may be available in a local college or business school in your area.

Look carefully at your self-analysis. What common threads move through the complete analysis? What subjects in school and jobs you held relate to one another? The more you know about yourself the easier it will be to develop the "I can do it" attitude that you need to succeed in your time-management program.

## Take Time to Conquer Your Fears and Worries

Frances V. looked at her watch. Nearly time to go home and the deadline approaching. The boss wanted this report for a meeting in the morning. Perspiration started to drip down over her forehead, her glasses started to get steamy, and she visualized in her mind how mad the boss would be when he received the news that the report would be late. Frances started blaming herself for starting the project too late, for not asking for help, and for even volunteering for the project in the first place. She spent a number of minutes with negative thoughts and rationalizations that only made the problem worse. Why add to your misery? Why not concentrate on what you must do at this time to handle your problems? Accomplishing the job is the most important thing. If you want to finish the job, take the time to decide on the next step to complete it.

Frances talked on the phone to her close friend in a similar job outside the company. She made an important set of decisions as a result of the conversation. She asked her boss for more help to get the report done for the next morning. Frances got the help and worked well into the night, but she accomplished her goals and met the deadline. If she had not asked for the help she would have increased her stress and worries to the point of exhaustion, thus depleting her energy to complete the work. Frances also practiced good management by communicating to her boss when she needed help. You will never get help unless you ask for it. In the selling field, you will never get the order unless you ask for it. It's far better to ask for the help to reach the deadline than it is to wait, work hard, miss the deadline, and then be forced to explain why you missed the deadline.

Fears and worries add up to stress. Stress can be avoided if you are willing to face the fact that even though you're organized, you can still miss deadlines or not meet certain obligations. Never feel guilty about being unable to do everything. You simply cannot expect to be able to do it all. Remember how we talked about Henry and his problems of "too many irons in the fire"? He tried to accomplish the impossible and added stress to his life. Be willing to say "NO" to stress. One way to do this is to admit what you cannot do. Sometimes you have to tell yourself, "I can't do it." You cannot please everyone. You cannot handle all the decisions in your company, in your family, or in your life. You are you, one and only. You can build a better you by taking stock of yourself. Avoid being everything for everyone. Cut stress by cutting out the impossible tasks.

The world can be an ocean of doubts, criticisms, jealousy, hate, bitterness, and cruelty. This ocean can still be navigated by you. You can be the captain of your ship. Just as the captain of the ship must plan the voyage completely before he leaves the dock, you must also realize that success in time management is really life management, and will not come to you quickly. You must plan for it and work for it. Give yourself the necessary time to reach your voyage goal. Success takes time just as anything good takes time. Not just busy-work time, but time for essentials to sail over the ocean of self-doubts and apprehensions in order to reach your port of call. One source of stress is people. The captain on his voyage must use people in order to get to his goal. You too must be able to handle people in order to be successful.

Sandra W. is an elementary school teacher in New Mexico. During a seminar she claimed that her biggest problem was dealing with other people. She felt she could handle the students without any problems. Her main source of stress resulted from a feeling that something was going to happen to her. She felt that her boss, the principal, would find her work unsatisfactory and fire her, or that a group of parents would get together and recommend that she be released from her job. Her time was consumed worrying about things that might never happen.

All of Sandra's fears were unfounded. She was an excellent teacher, perhaps the best teacher in the school, but she failed to believe in the most important product—herself. If you're good in your work you're not obligated to stay with one company or one school; you can go anywhere. Why waste that valuable energy worrying about things that will not happen? Concentrate your energies on constructive and positive thoughts. During the seminar Sandra set up a plan of action she would follow to cut down on her stress so she could go on with her life. She set up an appointment with her boss, the principal, and asked about her status as a teacher at the school. The principal gave her very high praise and told her that she was not only doing a good job, but that she was in line for the new position of assistant principal. Sandra was simply delighted. She discovered her fears unfounded, and with this new information she could get on with her work and even concentrate on becoming an assistant principal.

Jimmy U., the owner of a hardware store, found himself tied up in knots of stress because of his relationship with the fifteen people working in his store. He knew there was a problem, but he didn't want to take the time to solve it. Finally he held a staff meeting and asked his workers about this relationship. The central question discussed was: How can we develop a better working relationship together? The workers somewhat reluctantly stressed a theme that continued to come out over and over again—the lack of proper communication. The workers wanted to know how they were doing in their jobs. When they asked him a question, they received only a partial answer and not enough material or information to answer the question. Jimmy U. took notes of the meeting because he wanted to solve this problem for the good of the company.

Once the meeting was over, Jimmy thought about the meeting and the items discussed during the meeting. He was convinced that the lack of communication was a problem that he would work to resolve. He thought about how he had handled his employees in the past. Too often, he admitted to himself, he simply gave brief answers or undercommunicated to them. For example, he would say, "You are an average worker, so I will give you the average raise of 7 percent of your salary." Jimmy decided that he would make an effort to help more people grow within the organization by elaborating on his statements. For example, instead of saying "Your work is average," he would say, "Your work cannot be classified above average because you missed the deadline on the ABC Company account and you are habitually late in processing the purchasing forms. Now let's talk about how we can solve these problems together." Jimmy U. was determined to do all in his power to get the communications going so his company could be more successful. He took the action he needed to reduce the stress in his life.

One famous author likes to talk about a train trip he took a number of years ago. He had sat across the table from a married couple in the dining car. He had noticed that the woman was finding fault with everything in sight. The dining car was too hot. The dining car was overcrowded. The coffee was too weak. The hamburger was too well-done, and so on. This woman had a problem with everything. Finally the author had looked over at the man and had asked him about his work. The man had replied, "I'm an attorney, and my wife is in the manufacturing business." Since the woman had not looked like the business type, the author had asked about the goods she manufactured. The husband had replied, "She manufactures her own unhappiness." Stress is fed by people willing to manufacture their own unhappiness. Why look for the problems and the mistakes in the people, places, and things around you? Why not focus on the positive and constructive things in your life? The way you feel and act will bring about an important reaction in the other people working and living with you. If you see the positive things in others and focus on these positive things, people will enjoy and benefit from your company. How many people manufacture fears, worries, and negative thoughts each day? How many people give valuable time and effort to their problems instead of their opportunities? Why not focus on how you can do it rather than why you cannot? There are many ways to reach your goals, but you must have an attitude that is positive. Your attitude can make the difference between success and stress. You must give yourself a pat on the back.

In the average day your mind can either build you up or throw you down. For example, if you give yourself one thousand five hundred thoughts that you cannot do something, or worry about why you cannot do something, and during that same day you have twenty-five people tell you that you did a good job on something, you must now keep score. Which one is the winner, the positive or the negative thoughts? Of course, the negative thoughts will win each and every day, unless you concentrate and make an effort to manufacture your own positive inputs. Fill your life with positive thoughts and follow them up with positive actions to reach your goals. People enjoy being around and working with positive people. One very successful time manager was asked how he was able to accomplish so many things. He replied, "I'm in love with life, and right now we're on a honeymoon."

One doctor from Houston finds he can cut down on the stress in his profession by organization. Organization to help him do the things that he does the best. He makes certain that he hires assistants so that he can handle the most important operations and more difficult medical cases. This organization is also reflected in his business life. With the profits made in the medical business he invests in real estate with the aid of others. He hired three business assistants to handle his outside business deals. Although he makes the final decision on whether to buy or sell any real estate, he permits them to make the day-by-day decisions. He picks business assistants that are careful of his valuable time. They are very sparing with his time, but they make sure that he makes the important decisions. Do you manage yourself in your job, at home, and in your personal life so you can cut down on your stress? Make the necessary adjustments so that you can relax and accomplish even more.

Some people find good hobbies to help them relax and cut their stress to a minimum. Many people take to the golf course each weekend to unwind from their daily problems and take their frustrations out on the little white ball. All your hobbies should be as relaxing as possible; don't try to beat all comers and set the course record. Use the hobby to get away from the maddening crowd, far away from the normal problems and frustrations. Relax on the golf course, take a deep breath, enjoy the beautiful green grass, look at the beautiful trees, look at the breath-taking river, and enjoy what nature offers you. While you're relaxing on your day off, take the time to enjoy every moment. Each moment is unique so enjoy and utilize it to the fullest.

A source of stress can be the lack of ability to handle some of the members of your family. Do you let the children get you so upset that stress builds up? One mother of two small children found that it was stressful trying to please the children all the time. She made a decision to spend more time on some new activities each week. She decided that she would take some golf lessons and learn how to ski. She engaged a good friend to come to the house to care for the children so that she had some time of her own. She noticed that this time away from the children helped her in dealing with them. She also made a decision that the children would have to learn to adjust to her activities. She took them along when she went shopping, visiting, and so forth. She found that instead of centering all her time and her life on the children, she could develop a new schedule that would meet the needs of all the members of her family. You have a choice to accept the things that add to your stress or to make the changes to cut the stress to a minimum.

Another excellent way to put a stranglehold on your stress is to develop confidence in your ability to perform at a particular level in whatever activity is important to you. For example, I find that high school and college level students who are confident in themselves will perform better on tests and in their work. This past semester I had a number of new students in my college course who had never taken a college-level course. The reading, homework, and tests are usually difficult for students unaccustomed to college-level work. Nothing succeeds like success! Once the students found that they could pass a test, or could complete a difficult assignment, their stress was cut to a minimum and they could get on with the job at hand. This concept is also applicable to starting hobbies or new interests. Once you get the necessary information and skills to perform, you can accomplish your goals without the stress of the past. Develop that inner feeling of confidence in yourself.

You can build up a tremendous amount of stress by trying to be too nice to everyone and not looking out for the most important person: YOU. Let people know when you want something, whether it might be a raise on your job, a day off, another assistant, or help on an important job. The concept "the squeaky wheel will get the grease" applies here. For example, you gave an assistant a job to get some information you needed to finish a report for your boss. You requested the information two weeks ago, and you are still waiting for it. Now you ask the assistant for the information and you get a reply that the information has not arrived at the company. Now is the crucial time for action. You can take this answer and sit and wait while the stress builds up to the maximum level, or you can take some action to cut the stress to size. You are the manager of your time. Let's see how this situation could be handled.

> Time Manager: "Sue, I asked for the financial information for the XYZ report two weeks ago. Where is it?"
>
> Sue: "I sent for this information at the Acton Plant; it should be in shortly."
>
> Time Manager: "I need this information as soon as possible. Please get it for me today. I will not take NO for an answer any longer."
>
> Sue: "I will get on this immediately. I didn't know it was so urgent. You will have this by noon, O.K.?"
>
> Time Manager: "Thank you."

Notice how the time manager gave the problem right back to the assistant, rather than worrying, fretting, and perhaps taking it upon himself. Your work pile will increase if you try to accomplish the work for your whole department. Let each person perform his or her work. You have enough to do to handle your own work. A manager must lead, and if you take on lower-level work your leadership will suffer and so will your health. We will talk about leadership and what's needed to help leaders use their time most effectively in Chapter 17. In summary, your knowledge of your fears and worries are very important. Do something about them. Take the action you need to strangle rather than feed your stress. Stay positive about yourself and the special talents and abilities you possess. Develop the necessary outside interests and hobbies to recharge your batteries. Stand up to your problems and to other people who push you around. Put the pressure where it belongs to save you your time and energy.

# 13
# PLAN AHEAD

*Unclear planning* is another timewaster. How can you develop goals that are attainable for you and at the same time determine if these goals are "high payoff" for you? You must take the necessary time to plan for your career. You must take the necessary time to plan for your retirement, your next sales presentation, your next new product or service, or your next project at work. One manager in Mississippi finds that he can plan his goals much better when he determines what he wants to do and then lists all of the benefits on a sheet of paper. He wanted to order for his company a new machine that would produce almost double the units of the old machine. Instead of producing ten thousand units per day, the new machine would be able to produce almost twenty thousand units. On his benefit list he showed that the cost of each unit would decrease, that the company would save on labor costs and on material costs, and that the company would have more production time to produce the new product line. The salespeople could then take more orders and the delivery time of the products could be faster. Once he had listed the benefits, he investigated the cost involved in the purchase of the machine. Since the machine had a cost of $75,000 to purchase and install, and had a life of three years, the machine would have a cost to him of $25,000 per year. He found that the benefits of having this machine, such as the decrease in unit cost resulting in an increase in profit, would result in a dollar value of $32,000 per year and the net result would be a gain of $7,000. He decided it would pay to make this purchase of the machine.

*Proper planning and long-range planning can help you.* What do you want to accomplish? How do you plan to complete this goal? How much time will it take you to carry out this goal? Can you truly accomplish this goal without taking too much of your time for the other smaller jobs and duties? One very successful writer has a technique that all good time managers should consider: He determines what he wants to do and then shuts out everything and everyone that will interrupt him from accomplishing his duties. He is the most widely read novelist in the country and many of his books are made into films. In a recent interview on television he explained his very successful technique for writing his books. He locks himself into his special room and permits no visitors, no television, no telephone calls—literally no interruptions so he can get on with his work. He has his food sent into his room and even sleeps in the room. He stays in his room until the book is completed. Many of the ideas about the characters and themes of the book are in the embryonic stage when he goes into the room, but once he is able to give them full concentration, the story unfolds. I'm not necessarily recommending that this is a method that you should use, but it does show what can be completed when the proper planning of your time coordinates with the proper amount of full concentration time. Do you get enough of this full concentration time, when you're completely separated from your routine distractions? How can you develop a plan to permit more full concentration time for you? What members of your office or company can help you arrange this? Work on this as soon as possible to help save your most valuable resource, time, which should be used to fully zero in on your important problems.

Do you consider the obstacles and roadblocks to reaching your goals? If you want to learn to play tennis, it means setting aside time in your schedule in order to do this. It means hiring the right coach or tennis instructor and purchasing the equipment you will need to play this game. Too many goals aren't reached because of the lack of proper awareness of the multiple obstacles there will be along the way. The manager from Mississippi can expect many roadblocks in his pursuit of purchasing the machine. The treasurer of the company may not want to spend $75,000 for the machine at this time. The president of the company is more interested in new products than in producing more of the older products. Other people in management feel that too many of the existing production machines are being underutilized, and find it difficult to approve another machine for the company. Although you have strong feelings about your goal, problems will arise and you must be aware of these obstacles and be able to do something about them.

The manager from Mississippi must be willing to sell the fact that there will be an annual profit of $7,000 with the use of new machines. He must also convince the treasurer of the company that this $75,000 investment will pay off for the company. He must sell the president of the company on the fact that the profits on each unit produced with the new machine will be increased. The president might be looking toward new products for the company to keep up with the new and emerging markets. The manager may be required to convince the management that the new machine will be utilized to the maximum, unlike many machines purchased in the past. There are a number of important considerations to ponder when you develop your goals. Your goals will only be as successful as the necessary time you spend in planning to reach these goals. On the next two pages you will find the necessary goal forms, which include your goal title, the obstacles and roadblocks, the solutions, the rewards and benefits, and the method of keeping score.

Illustration 8 is a sample goal-setting plan of action for someone who wants to stop smoking. Illustration 9 is for you to use for your own special goal.

Notice in Illustration 8 that there is a target date for completion of each solution. In thirty days the smoker planned on cutting down to one-half pack of cigarettes. In sixty days he would stop smoking completely. You will have a much better chance of reaching your goals if all these elements of goal-setting are completely spelled out for you. Setting your goals is decision-making in a true sense. You're

**GOAL:**
  TO STOP SMOKING

**OBSTACLES AND ROADBLOCKS:**
  Breaking a six-year habit

  Tolerating smoking by others once I stop

  Keeping my smoker friends

  Putting on weight

| **SOLUTIONS:** (BE SPECIFIC. LIST EACH STEP IN DETAIL AS TO HOW YOU WILL ACCOMPLISH GOALS AND OVERCOME OBSTACLES.) | TARGET DATES |
|---|---|
| Cutting down to less than one-half pack a day | 30 days |
| Cutting down gradually until I stop completely | 60 days |
| Trying to avoid social situations with heavy smoking | 60 days |
| Explaining to my smoker friends I wanted to stop for personal reasons | 60 days |
| Starting an exercise program | 45 days |

**REWARDS AND BENEFITS:**
  Protect my health

  Save money

  Save on my health insurance

**METHOD OF KEEPING SCORE:**

| DATE | PROGRESS TO DATE |
|---|---|
| Feb. 1 | Cut my smoking to one-half pack a day |

**ILLUSTRATION 8. GOALS PLAN OF ACTION**

deciding what you want to do while you're consuming your most important resource—your TIME. Take a look in your local paper and every week you will see hundreds of people starting their own businesses. Many of these businesses are retail stores or service businesses. How many of these business owners take the necessary time to write out a clear, definite set of goals for their businesses? By using the Goals Plan of Action, Illustration 9, they would get their business started on the right track from the point of view of their goals. It would help them become aware of the problems that might come up in the

```
GOAL:


OBSTACLES AND ROADBLOCKS:




SOLUTIONS:  (BE SPECIFIC. LIST EACH STEP IN
             DETAIL AS TO HOW YOU WILL
             ACCOMPLISH GOALS AND                TARGET
             OVERCOME OBSTACLES.)                DATES







REWARDS AND BENEFITS:



METHOD OF KEEPING SCORE:
    DATE                      PROGRESS TO DATE
```

**ILLUSTRATION 9. GOALS PLAN OF ACTION**

business. Most small-business people know what they want to do in their business to make it succeed. Clearly spelling out your goals will help you in the future because you will have a direction and a pacesetter. A well-developed goal makes you try even harder to use your time to the maximum.

Use your goals to accomplish your present desires and needs. Rhonda C. had an office administrator's position within a medium-sized dental office. She decided to take some college courses in business to help her in her job. One of the first courses she took was a course in Personnel Management. As part of the course, I assigned a term paper on some phase of personnel management, and I asked all students to develop and write that paper on a subject that could give them an advantage in their careers or their present position. Rhonda wrote a very interesting paper on the need to communicate in the office, and how the lack of proper communication can affect the overall morale and the effectiveness of the organization. I found out later in the course that Rhonda had given one copy of the paper to her boss. He had been so happy with the paper that he had given her a bonus right away. The boss had been pleased to see one of his employees utilizing her education in a manner that brought excellent results for the company. Do you presently use your education, your reading, your seminars and extra training to help your company? By helping your company you will be making inroads on your pursuit of your long-term goals. Try to make all of your work and assignments as relevant to your own interests as possible.

How can you get more out of your time? Right now trying to obtain the maximum out of your time is entirely up to you. Some business organization planners foresee the possibility of a large computer located in a central position of the company to be used by all employees to give them a list of work assignments for that particular workday. The supervisor would receive the new list of orders to fill for the day. The manager would receive the latest list of important assignments in his or her department. The assignments would be based on the very latest goals and objectives of the company.

Until a computer can help you manage your time you must try to manage time successfully by doing one thing at a time. A bright, perceptive efficiency-expert developed an important idea that helped a well-known steel company become the leader in its field. That idea was a simple one: have each manager in the company make a list of seven things they want to complete that day. Then, first thing in the morning, they should start on item one and work on it until it's finished. Then they should move on to item two, continuing in this manner until it's time to go home. Even if they do not finish all seven items, they must keep working on that list until they finish each item. This new approach worked very well for the managers at this company—so well in fact, that the managers told their foremen and supervisors to use it and the company became extremely successful. Many of the employees were using this system every working day and it became a working style for them. This simple idea made them more efficient and cut their workload in half, because they were sticking to certain jobs to get them completed so they could go on to the next important job.

*Spend the necessary time to plan your time.* What do you want to accomplish tomorrow in your job? Take the necessary time you need to plan your day completely. Some managers find that they need to take thirty minutes daily to fully plan the days. How do you use each morning? How do you successfully use the afternoon? Do you include your associates in your time planning? Do you take advantage of your assistant's talents and abilities in your planning? In order to plan successfully you should have a full understanding of all the resources available to you. Do you use all those technical, mechanical, and human resources available to you? Do you take the time to plan for future events? One manager in Massachusetts tries to use a certain amount of time each day to prepare for the future advancements within his department. One major electronics company has a full department of people planning a five-year plan for the company. This plan will help them determine the best way to use their time and resources for the best return on investment. Good planning will give you the best possible return on investment.

*Draw a weekly plan and put it to work.* One time manager from Wellington, Ohio, finds she can accomplish more work when she spends Friday afternoons carefully and completely planning for the next week. Her first list is simply a listing of everything that needs to be completed. Her next list is similar to the writer's redraft of an article. It is made up of things to do in order of importance of "high payoff" for the company. The next stage of her planning is making a delegation sheet whereby she determines the people in the office who can best handle each job. Friday afternoon is the key planning day to outline her goals for the next week.

*Your goals can help you accomplish more.* Ed N. is a very

successful sales manager for a life insurance company, and he credits his success to proper goal-setting not only for himself, but for his other salespeople as well. He sits down with each salesperson and talks person-to-person with him or her about personal goals. One salesperson wanted a boat. Another wanted to purchase a large house at the seashore. Another wanted to put $10,000 in the bank to collect interest. Ed wrote down each goal and every week he would ask that salesperson what they accomplished that week to help them reach a little closer to their goal. Once a salesperson reached this goal, another goal was developed to take its place.

Successful companies set five- and ten-year plans. These plans include the new products they plan to develop and market in the future, and how they will compete with their competition in the future. Do you have a goal for this week? Or for this month? This year? For five years? Your goals are really decisions in the true sense. You're deciding what you want from your time. You have the same amount of minutes and hours per day as everyone else. Why not develop realistic goals to make each second count for you? Your goals can make the difference.

*"I'm much too busy to consider my career goals."* David W. was recently discharged from the military and wanted to find a police chief's position in a small community near his New Hampshire home. Shortly after he arrived home, an opening developed in a town close to him. He started to write a résumé to help get an interview for the job. He found that he had both military and civilian experience, but he had a difficult time trying to tie all this information together to compile a successful résumé. He decided to turn the job over to a résumé writer and career counselor. The career counselor read all the related information about David—his civilian and military jobs, all of his awards and miscellaneous information. By reviewing all this material the career manager found that his work experience was a series of basic police training programs, investigatory work, and supervisory work. The career manager showed David W. that his experience, although in both the civilian and military sectors, had a step-by-step process that suited

him well for the police job. David, like so many other people, tended to downplay his skills, talents, and abilities. Take the necessary time to review what you have accomplished so far, and what you must do now to reach your next goals.

# 14
# REWARDS
# ARE IMPORTANT

Many of us work on certain jobs or goals because we want the rewards. The student works hard to get the top grade in a certain subject. The salesperson works diligently to sell a large account and to receive a large commission. The baseball player practices his hitting so that he can help his team and increase his salary. The entertainer works hard on a new act to increase her popularity and bookings. The artist tries hard to develop new art techniques to increase art sales. The writer researches and develops new ideas to reach the best-seller list. Notice that all of these goals have a reward. The jobs and goals must be realistic as well as the rewards meaningful. One very successful time manager with many successes to his credit made this comment with regard to rewards and time management: "Every day I try and do something I enjoy. Life is too short for misery. We have to be selfish at times, but flexible enough so people will like us. There must be a balance between work and pleasure, between work and rewards. That's where good time management comes in. The selection of rewards is extremely important."

It's one thing to give yourself a reward for getting a long-term goal like a college degree after a number of years of work, but how about the short-term jobs you accomplish each day? Do you give yourself daily rewards? What about that short job you accomplished the other day? What about painting the back porch? What about that hard-to-do job you finally finished for your relative? Do you take care of the daily jobs and the daily rewards? Why not reward the most important person: YOU.

Rewards, just like goals, are individual. One of my friends will not watch television unless he spends time with his children and a certain amount of work in his workshop. A woman from Hawaii told me she is working hard on a new newsletter for writers, and she will not take any full rewards (like a trip) until she gets the newsletter in a profitable position. She presently gives herself small rewards for small achievements; for instance, when an extra batch of subscriptions comes in. An entrepreneur from Maine, when he has a very good week at his art business, goes on a shopping spree and buys clothes for himself. Sometimes the clothes are not needed, but he feels that the spree's an opportunity to be good to himself. Good rewards make the hard work worthwhile for you.

In the business field rewards play a very important role in the success of the organization. The organization will succeed when the employees are motivated to do the very best job possible for the company. In selling, for example, the compensation is set up on a commission-plus-salary program. The salesperson will receive $150 per week for salary for example, plus a commission of 10 percent on the total sales. The $150 is just salary, and to become more motivated, the salesperson must work extra hard to get the extra commission. The bonus is the carrot at the end of the stick to motivate and reward the salesperson to work a little harder.

Another reward that works very well in business is awarding a special trip to the top salesperson within the organization. A trip to a warm spot during an especially cold time of year is an example. Still another method of rewarding someone is electing him or her to a particular club or group that honors special accomplishments. One such organization for the baseball world is the Hall of Fame. The major companies selling life insurance will appoint their top salespeople into the Million-Dollar Round Table, a select group of people who have sold over one million dollars of life insurance over a period of time. This recognition gives them added prestige, and it can be added to their business cards so that their customers or their potential customers will be made aware that they're dealing with a top-notch salesperson. People want to deal with successful people, and by telling people about your successes you will help yourself reach your goals.

Just as the business world developed hundreds of different compensation plans to reward their employees, you must search for the best possible rewards for you. Here is a list of rewards that many people use. Perhaps you can find one or two even more potential rewards that you could incorporate into your life. Rewards might include:

Vacation trips
Watching pro sports on television
Tennis
Golf
Hunting
Fishing
Hiking
Camping
Bicycling
Pleasure trips in car
Shopping for yourself
Introduction into special organization
Pleasure trip by train

Now pick the reward that appeals to you so you can forge ahead in your social life, your career, your job, or your business. Many successful time managers find that the rewards help pave the way for greater rewards. For example, one popular radio personality and journalist takes regular vacations to unusual countries as his reward for working hard. A recent vacation took him to Israel, and the trip gave him enormous ideas and a much better understanding of the Middle East. By taking the time away from his normal everyday life, he saw many new trends and happenings, and the creative juices started to flow for new ideas. These experiences were related to his audience, and added to his show. Take the time to treat and reward yourself; you deserve it.

You deserve your own rewards. It matters very little what occasion you want to reward, whether it's finishing a long and difficult course, learning how to ski, completing a grueling week at your job, or completing a difficult and long assignment. Take your reward—you deserve it. I have one client who continues to inform me of all the reasons why she should not reward herself. She feels that she should spend the money for her rewards on her family, her numerous sons, daughters, and grandchildren. Her family did not complete the job or assignment, so I explained that she should take care of herself first. You are a very important person, so you want to take good care of yourself.

A successful businessman who is president of a service club was recently interviewed on television. He was asked to comment on the main reason or reasons for his excellent success in business. He felt that his membership in his service club made the difference in his life. He went on to say that all of his time is very precious to him, but spending time each week at the club paid dividends for him. The speakers at each weekly meeting delivered messages which served as stimulators and motivators for all members. This gentleman felt that each meeting was a reward in itself. Do you receive enough rewards to remotivate yourself to do even more in the future? Put yourself in the environment that will offer you the rewards that are meaningful to you.

# 15
# CLOSE THE
# TIME DRAINS AND ADD
# HOURS TO EACH DAY

*Conserving your time is very important.* All of us are allotted 1,440 minutes each day. We have approximately six hundred minutes each day if we take the normal ten-hour day. Do you consume these six hundred minutes on essential activities? Do you find yourself wasting many minutes on jobs that could be handled by others? Your job success will be determined by your proper selection of the right job at the correct time. Consider the way you consume your time similar to that of spending money: the shopper wants to get the most for his dollar; you want to get the highest return on those six hundred working minutes you spend daily. Make the minutes count.

In order to add hours to each day you must try to cut those ten- and fifteen-minute clumps of time that add up fast. Do you find yourself doing jobs you know have a very low payoff for you? Do you find that little drops of wasted time, the fifteen- and twenty-minute drops of time, add up during the day to substantial time losses? Successful time managers have the ability to analyze their own time and work habits. One time manager from New York found that his travel time, both his time for the company and his own personal commuting time, was very excessive. He made two decisions to cut down on this wasted time. First, he delegated some of his travel to his assistant. He could spend the newly created time to do the planning he needed in his job. Secondly, he purchased a house closer to his job to cut his commuting time from two hours each day to only forty minutes.

An attorney from Massachusetts, Ray V., found that his procrastination on both the small and the large jobs caused him to waste valuable time. When his clients asked him about why a certain job was not completed for them he would be forced to give them an excuse to satisfy them. He found himself spending more and more of his time trying to come up with excuses and rational explanations to protect his procrastination. He determined that his procrastination was his own attempt to give himself more time to do certain jobs and cases. He also felt the procrastination was the result of taking on too many outside activities. He was trying to do too many things for too many people. He cut his outside activities to a bare minimum and then found the necessary time and energy to meet his daily work obligations.

Use your peak times to help close the time drains. Sereana M. is a real morning person. She gets up very early each day. Even on her days off she continually gets up with the dawn. She finds that she can handle many routine jobs early in the morning long before she goes off to work as an interior designer. She also finds the morning is the best time for her at work. Many of her very creative ideas on interior design come to her during the hours before eleven o'clock in the morning.

Olga D. is just the opposite. She finds that the most important and effective time in her day is after four o'clock in the afternoon. It's not unusual to get an evening telephone call from Olga at your home. She is in the office although it's eight o'clock in the evening, working on her job. Each person has particular peak times for effective work. Do you know and use yours effectively?

The time drains are open not only on the job but also during your leisure time. One woman from Detroit, an insomniac, spent a great deal of time just moving and tossing in her bed. One evening she got a bright idea: why not develop a program for all the other insomniacs in the Detroit area? She wrote a program for an evening tour of the city of Detroit, starting at midnight. The tour included a concert starting around midnight and going to one o'clock in the morning. Next the tour went to an all-night restaurant, and then visited an all-night radio show. A tour of a large radio station was included as well. The tour may prove very lucrative for its founder, especially at a price of $100 per person. This example proves that time is really money after all.

Another example of closing a time drain is the way an American hostage decided to use his time. In November, 1979, Richard Queen was one of the hostages taken by the Iranian students. Since he was a recent graduate of a well-known university, he decided to pretend to himself that he was still at the university doing his studying. He buried himself in books to keep his mind off the fact he was being held hostage. He read hundreds of books during the eight months he was held hostage. At one point, his roommate asked him to play cards. Richard agreed to play cards but made it clear he could play cards only during the afternoon and perhaps in the evening, but during the morning he would concentrate on his reading. He had the ability to say "No" to playing cards for the full day. If you can't say "No" to the drains or potential drains on your time you will find yourself overloaded with work or activities, with little time to do them well.

One industrial company found itself squeezed by the recession. It needed more sales in order to keep the business profitable. In order to do this the company designed a sales plan to call on more customers. The order went out: simply pound on more doors and give your customers better services. Stay positive, hungry, optimistic; and take the needed initiative. The program was needed because before the recession the salespeople had been simply order-takers; if there were shortages in certain materials they accepted only certain orders and rejected others. Just as this industrial company was forced to start a new program to add hours to each day, you must also start new programs to monitor and control the time drains in your own life. Do you get into habits like the salespeople, and wait for someone to call the order to you? Do you make the extra effort to give your company, your family, or your job the extra touch you need to reach your goals? Do you find yourself sliding away from top-level jobs, only to do other lower-level jobs that give you very little satisfaction and use precious time? This industrial company added more hours to all their employees' days by keeping someone on the phone on the sales desk from 7 A.M. to 7 P.M. No one worked overtime. The salespeople juggled their hours; some started earlier in the day while others started later as required.

Good time management might mean just getting the commitment from other workers to help you reach certain goals. People want to feel that their talents, abilities, and skills are working to help the company. Their talents, abilities, and skills are important to them, and they want to use them to help you and the organization. Just as the industrial company must periodically set up a campaign to motivate its workers and salespeople to do a little bit extra, you must also consider developing your own campaign to make the best use of your time. Some time managers use different signs in their offices to keep them in tune with their current time-management campaign. Others use posters to keep them on track with their goals for success. Stay on track to reach new goals.

One very successful time manager from Michigan found that his key to successful time management was self-management. He learned that by taking advantage of the skills and talents he possessed at each stage of his life, he could stretch out his time. For example, he found in his twenties that he had a difficult time relating to people. He lacked the confidence to communicate the way he really wanted to. So he used his twenties to get the hard work accomplished in his career. Now that he is in his forties he not only can accomplish more work, but he possesses the maturity that gives him an advantage in working closely with other people. You have a special background. You have a special and unique personality. You are blessed with certain personal habits. These personal habits are both beneficial and detrimental to you. The manager from Michigan took the necessary time to understand himself and this understanding helped him use his talents and time better. You can add hours to your day by getting to really know the most important product: YOU. You are not working for the ABC company, or the XYZ company. You are working for yourself. You are selling your skills, talents, and abilities for a certain amount of money per week, or per month, depending on how you get paid. For this pay, you are accomplishing certain jobs, within a certain time period. You want to make use of this valuable time. You only have one career. You must take advantage of this time by using it wisely and concentrating on work that will bring you the largest rewards.

Joe L. found himself doing a number of jobs in his business. Many of the jobs were routine and unrelated to his job in production of electronic transistors. He made a decision to concentrate more on the jobs he felt he had the most talent and skill to complete, such as checking the quality control of the products and scheduling the production for his department. He delegated the other jobs to other people within his department and found he accomplished more work. Do you try to do the work you feel you are most confident of completing? Why do you try to do jobs outside of your field of competence? A school principal from New Hampshire found he was spending almost twelve hours a week on odd jobs around his house. Although he didn't mind doing these jobs, he felt he could make better use of his time, so he hired someone to handle these jobs for him, leaving him time to write articles for professional journals. Are you getting your money's worth from your time—all of your time?

Another way to add hours to your day is to evaluate your ability to accomplish and handle certain jobs and assignments. Be honest with yourself. Do you take too long handling a particular job because you lack the specialized knowledge you need or because your education in this area is limited? You may simply need additional training to keep up. Hundreds of thousands of people are now going back to school to keep up with the changing times. Companies are finding that their employees need further education to keep up with the competitive times. One vice-president of a radio network is presently spending every Friday in class studying for a master's degree in business. Over five hundred thousand business managers per year take some type of business and management training program, whether it takes the form of seminars or full two-year programs.

Many companies not only pay the tuition, but also consider the schoolwork part of the employee's job. The companies and students in these management and business programs find that the investment in education is the best possible investment. Many people who are successful in their fields today will find themselves obsolete in ten years or less without some continuing education in the field. If you find that you need some additional education to help you reach new opportunities in your job, you might be able to attend your local high school during an evening program. Perhaps you have a vocational school in your area that offers courses for you. Another very important source of education is the local community college. Some community colleges offer a huge variety of courses from special interest courses to job-related programs to help you in your career. One of our local community colleges offers such courses as electronics, medical transcribing, art for industry, nursing, engineering, drafting, business management, secretarial skills, travel, criminal justice, education, management development, and liberal arts. The special interest courses include papier mâché, mosaic art, wood sculpture, watercolor techniques, introduction to life-work planning, adventures in attitudes, the relaxation class, wine appreciation, dream workshop, ballroom dance, and numerous others. As you can see, the courses are available to you to help you keep up on your education. Once you determine what courses you would like to take, go over the courses with your boss to discover if these courses can be paid for by the company and will be relevant to you and your company. The education and training you want might be right within your neighborhood.

Good time management is practicing where you need it the most. Susan B. held an acting administration manager's position in a large government office. She was an excellent administrator and handled the clerical paperwork extremely well. She also came up with a number of time-saving methods to process the numerous government forms. Susan disliked the numerous meetings she was required to attend and even more, the weekly meeting she was required to run for her own staff. Speaking in front of a group was not a job she enjoyed, but she accepted this as part of her job.

A seminar became available in the local area on "How to Run a Successful Meeting" and she decided to attend. She picked up a number of ideas and techniques, but a common thread ran through the seminar—successful communication requires practice and more practice. She decided that she would accept more invitations to speak at various clubs and organizations to sharpen her speaking ability. She found soon that she eagerly looked forward to her own meetings and felt a new feeling of satisfaction in her job. Do you take the necessary time and effort to work on your weaknesses?

Another one of the best ways to increase the hours in your day is to review your reading program. Do you spend too much time reading? Do you spend too much time on information with little value to you and your organization? Too many people feel they must read everything that comes to their attention. Try to read only the important information that will help to do your job better. One time manager from Washington, D.C., saves time by limiting his reading of the morning mail. He will only read the information that he determines to be the most important. The other papers, advertisements, and miscellaneous items are thrown out. You have numerous items competing for your time and your reading attention from the moment you get up in the morning until you retire at night. Be very selective in what you read. Avoid the habit of trying to read every item you receive. Some time managers find that by reading the topic sentence in each paragraph they get the important points. Sometimes you can read the first and last paragraphs to get the summary and the important points of a report.

While reading, take the opportunity to get involved with the subject. Write in the margins of the report. Underline certain key words or phrases. Summarize the report in one sentence if possible. How does this report relate to you? The famous philosopher Francis Bacon once said, "Some books are to be tasted, other books are to be fully consumed." In the same manner, some of your reading will be essential, while other reading can be skimmed. Some time managers will save precious time by subscribing to publications that review other magazines and publications. For example, instead of reading seven or eight business magazines to stay up with your field, subscribe to a newsletter that reviews all these magazines and presents them in a condensed newsletter. Can you have someone else read certain information and present it to you? Sometimes managers delegate reading to others to help them save time. Some of the best-selling books are being put on cassette tapes so that people can listen to the books while doing other things. One time manager from Connecticut found that he could keep up with the best sellers by listening to them during the two hours he commuted each day to work.

Do you read certain books and publications simply by habit? Why do you read these books or publications? Try a different book for variety. For example, most of the books I read are nonfiction. Last month, I took a novel out of the library and enjoyed it. The novel opened up many new ideas for me, ideas and concepts I would never have developed with the usual books and publications I read. The novel was full of everything: people, sex, happiness, family problems, and life problems. The book was fast-moving and full of suspense and drama. I felt I grew by reading this exciting novel. By adding new books and publications to your reading program you will also add variety.

*Can you use your commuting time better?* Many people live in the suburbs of America and work in the major cities, and a tremendous amount of time is spent commuting. Many workers in the Connecticut area find it takes about 90 minutes to commute to work and at least 90 minutes to return. Many workers spend at least two hours commuting and many three or more hours. Can you use this time more creatively? One time manager from California finds that driving to and from work while listening to self-motivating tapes on his tape recorder gives him a real lift and a good feeling about using his time. A train commuter from Maine finds that during the three hours of commuting each day he does his reading of the latest business and trade journals, and much of the routine paperwork he cannot find time to do during the normal work day. An administrative manager of a large hospital outside of Boston finds that the car pool in which she belongs is an excellent source of ideas for her job.

The accountant will give her a different answer about a particular situation or problem than will the computer specialist who is also a member of the car pool. A teacher at the college level uses her commuting time to plan the next lecture or the very best questions to ask on the final exam.

Manager Bill V. in Pittsburgh finds that commuting time enables him to evaluate the success or lack of success of the day's work. He uses this time to ask himself what he really accomplished during the day; yes, it was a busy day, but did I work on the really vital and important work I must concentrate on to advance and succeed in my work? Just as a football coach will run the game film at the end of the football game to show the players what they did right and wrong during the game, Bill V. looks at his performance to determine just where he spent his time during the day. He found when examining one Monday that he simply had had too many drop-in visitors. During the commuting time he developed a strategy to defend against drop-in visitors. Do you review your day's work record to see if you can make it even more time efficient the next day? Your commuting time can give you the opportunity to do this.

Another way of developing your full use of commuting time is to use the idea of Joe K. of New Hampshire. He will repeat to himself motivating statements on how he can accomplish certain goals for that day. He will also practice to himself what he will say to certain employees and clients in meetings he has planned for that day. He keeps a pad of paper with him at all times during the commute just in case he comes up with an idea to help him in his job. He finds that some of his best ideas come to him during the morning drive to work. Your commuting time can be very valuable to you if you're willing to use it correctly.

Can you get up an hour earlier each day to increase your time? This can be difficult at first. One of my clients found that he was able to add an hour to each day by getting up a half-hour earlier in the morning and going to bed a half-hour later at night. He used this time to do some planning for his clothing business. Adding hours to your day might mean looking at your normal day in a different way. You can add or delete certain hours to help you improve your time management. Just one hour each day will give you three hundred sixty-five extra hours a year. The extra three hundred sixty-five hours will give you over fifteen extra days during the year to attain the extra things you want to accomplish.

*Use your "quiet time" to get more time mileage.* One executive from Alabama found his time running out and his work piling higher and higher. One day he took a survey of his time only to find that in order to get more from his time he needed "quiet time" in the office to do his important work. He found that the phone calls and visitors started to slow down around 12:15 to 1:30 P.M. each day, so he decided that instead of joining the others for lunch at this time he would use this valuable time for his work periods. He went to lunch at a different time. Do you have any time during your day that you can use for this "quiet time"? You might try to reschedule your time to use it to your advantage. You might argue that going to lunch with others in the office is of more benefit to you than the "quiet time." If you feel this to be true you may want to use the "quiet time" program once or twice a week. Get into this habit—it will work well.

*Use the full opportunities you have right now.* Never feel that the work you are presently doing is of little importance to you or to the firm. As you move up in the organization you will find changes in the work and the quantity of your work. At a recent time-management seminar a young lady raised her hand. She asked, "What do you do when you're way down on the list of your boss's priorities?"

Everyone in the world of work at one time or another has experienced the feeling that the boss is putting them on the bottom or near the bottom of his or her list of priorities. When you're in this situation, take advantage of your time to do various jobs and assignments to round out your experience and training. There are a number of very important advantages to having the spare time to do your work. While waiting for your boss, you can take advantage of the time by doing necessary reading, inquiring about other departments, or getting the next assignment started. The boss will see you when he is ready, so you must continue with other work. Try not to fragmentize your work. Move from one job to another to avoid interrupting your work. When you concentrate on doing your job a little better each day, you will find that your problems will change; the boss will want to see you *too much* because you will have become a very important person within the organization. Your time management will pay off for you.

*Is the information available?* Too much time and effort is spent finding out additional information about a subject when the information is available in the local public library. One research director for a large bank marketing company finds himself with many different research projects each day. Before he accepts a new project, he always asks this very important question: "Is this information available already?" When the information is readily available he will use it instead of wasting his own precious time and energy. Sometimes the information you need may not be available in the form of written information but will be available through tapping the most important resource within your company—your own employees. The sales manager should know more about the uses of your product or service than any other person in the company. Your personnel manager should have the latest information about the cost of the fringe benefit program in your company. The various managers know most about their departments in your company and it's up to you to utilize their valuable knowledge, experience, and skills. Use this valuable information.

New ideas can open many new hours in each day. Far too many people continue to hold tightly to old, tired, worn-out methods and techniques, and the final result is excessive waste of that limited resource—their time. I spoke to a very capable artist in Maine recently. He has a very large inventory of oil paintings. He has piles of paintings, some of them dating back to over ten years ago. Right now his business is slow. I asked him if there were other ways to sell the paintings rather than by showing them next to his van while he painted. I asked him about hiring an agent to help sell the paintings. One approach would be to give the agent a certain percentage of the total sales. If the agent, for example, sold a painting for $500 with a commission of 10 percent, the artist would receive $450 and the agent $50. The agent would be giving the artist the "multiplication effect" by reaching out to customers and potential customers the artist could not reach himself. The artist, like so many others, rebelled against the idea because he didn't know any art agents. I suggested that he contact other friends in the same field and ask how they hired their agents. Or he could send their agents a few representative samples of his work and keep sending these out until he found a suitable agent. To be successful in art, you must get as many people as possible to view your work. Let people know what you can do for them. Open up new ideas to reach your goals.

New computer ideas are now being developed to help the harried American executive use time better. The computer has been developed to the extent that too much data is being generated to the people in the world of work. All the information to make decisions is available. The main problem is time. There is too little time to gather all the information for use in decision-making. How can you simplify this information-gathering? One new idea being introduced is called "graphic data." It converts written information, including figures, into a figure or a graph to simplify it. The graph can be in different colors to show changes in previous months or years. Let's say, for example, the computer in your company develops monthly reports showing your accounts-receivable listing and the listing of monies owed to you by your customers buying on credit. One question you want to answer is, how old are the accounts-receivable accounts? It would be one thing to read it from the computer report and another thing to look at it with a graphic data system like the one in Illustration 10.

Notice how the graphic data gives you the information in a clear, easy-to-understand manner. The Chinese have a well-known saying that shows how clearly they understand and value the graphic methods: *a picture is worth a thousand words*. A good

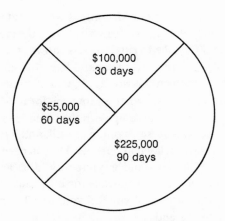

**ILLUSTRATION 10. ACCOUNTS RECEIVABLE BALANCE**

example of this concept is a doctor trying to explain a difficult procedure to a patient or a member of the patient's family. It would be one thing to try to explain the procedure or operation in words and quite another one to draw an illustration of the procedure on a sheet of paper. A teacher will discuss certain points about a subject and then use the blackboard to clarify the work even more.

You can aid your company or organization when you clearly understand and use all the information you receive. The best computer reports are useless unless your worker understands the information and how the information affects the company and organization. Use graphic data when dealing with difficult subject matter to help in your understanding. You will thereby gain more time.

*"That idea was tried before; it will never work now."* In order to fully reach your own goals and to save some of your precious time, new ideas are required. Your new ideas can be a threat to others, however—not only members of your own family, but also your

associates. Be persistent. Your idea might work, and in the event the idea fails to work, you will have grown by trying the idea. One woman in New Jersey had the idea to run business shows in various shopping malls all over the country. Her husband liked the idea, but told her about the many problems associated with it. The idea was put on the back burner until they had more time for it. Months went by and finally someone else came up with the same idea. The idea was finally tried by the New Jersey woman as well, and it was successfully merchandised, but the delay had hurt her. Do you permit other people and negative reactions to stand in your way? Just as the successful salesperson must accept three refusals for his product before he gets an order from the customer, if you feel your idea has merit, stay with your idea right to the end.

Another good example of the need to stick with a potential idea is Thomas Edison's invention of the storage battery. He would start early each day and do one experiment after another until one worked. He would number his experiments, and when he reached ten thousand he would call them a series. He did eight series before he came up with the successful experiment for the storage battery. Thomas Edison used his time well, staying on the most important job, not moving to other experiments, and being persistent even after many failures. If you have a good idea, stay with it; use your time to make it succeed.

*"It sounds like a good idea, but I thought we were doing this already. . . ."* One time manager, Chet F., in New Jersey, found that even after he had asked his employees for suggestions for new ways to make their jobs easier, new ways to increase production, new ways to improve quality, or new ways to cut costs, very few employees came forward with suggestions. He had a meeting with his employees and told them of their importance to the firm. At the end of the meeting he had the employees fill out forms asking questions about their jobs and the attitudes they had about their roles in the company.

Chet F. found that many of the employees felt that their ideas were already in operation in the plant or would be implemented in the near future. Many workers did not want to be in a position whereby their suggestions seemed too simple. In short, they tended to downgrade their own ideas. Chet F. then developed a suggestion system which involved additional meetings with supervisors of the company. These meetings opened up the opportunities for suggestions—even the simple, obvious ideas—for the benefit of the company. He found that this program also made the managers, supervisors, and workers take more pride and have real involvement in their work.

The federal government has developed a suggestion program that must be implemented by all of their subcontractors. This program is concerned with finding newer and better ways to save time and money for the company working in a contractual relationship with the government. When a worker makes a suggestion that will save money for the company, his or her suggestion is carefully screened and discussed by a panel of specialists. He or she is paid a certain sum of money depending on the total amount of dollars saved by the suggestion. The government has used this program for many years because it saves both time and money. Do you get the right amount of suggestions from others in your job and at home?

New ideas can give you extra hours in your day. Just recently I helped run a seminar on time management for the municipal department heads of a large city. During the seminar we talked about how new ideas can help you do your job better. I gave some examples of creative ideas and how these ideas could help managers perform at a higher level on their jobs. One example was the use of a newsletter to communicate to the workers and customers of a particular department. The newsletter could be used as a communication tool to reach others. A few days after the seminar I read in the newspaper that one department head had developed a newsletter for his department. This newsletter would now save some of his valuable time. Instead of writing numerous individual letters to other members of the department, he could let the newsletter become the central news source. You can find new ideas right within your office, your organization, or your home—right within your grasp.

*Look at your job and challenges in a unique manner.* What is the usual way to handle this problem? What has been used in the past to handle certain jobs? One very successful owner of a growing advertising agency found that looking at each problem in a unique, fresh way gave her an advantage over her competitors. She is now a millionaire because of her ability to use her time in a creative manner to reach out for ideas not currently available. A number of studies show that the "brain-storming" techniques for developing ideas are not the top idea-developers today. One of the very latest techniques is to take a problem and continue to explain it over and over again until you can develop one or two sentences to summarize the problem and a solution. In order to perfect this technique, you must take the necessary time to practice creative thinking.

*Use outside consultants and suppliers to save you time.* I worked as a personnel manager for a company that I found lacked a safety program. The company needed a safety program to help them to conform to the OSHA (Occupational Safety and Health Act) and other governmental regulations for the safety of the workers. I started to do the research to develop the program and found the name of the insurance company that handled our worker compensation insurance. I called our insurance agent and received a tremendous amount of help from her as well as from the carrier for our insurance. I also found that since we were members of the Small Business Association, they would provide us with help and much useful information to start our safety program. The federal government also makes available millions of pamphlets and bulletins on safety and how a business may conform to the OSHA regulations. By the utilization of the insurance agent, the insurance carrier, the Small Business Association, and the information directly available from the federal government, I was able to develop an outstanding safety program in a short period of time. If I had tried to develop the program myself without using these free consultants, I would have used much more time.

In the same company we had a large fleet of trucks and trailers we used to pick up and deliver our paper products. I noticed that each month we would send a check to a consultant whom the company had hired years ago to help us with the trucking and transportation problems in the company. Our main office in New Jersey was concerned that we were losing money in the trucking portion of our business. I called the consultant on the phone and set up a meeting with him to discuss our trucking problems. I learned in our discussions that his firm had a computer that could calculate whether or not we were making a profit or loss in our trucking. The computer also showed which trucks and truck drivers were making a profit for the firm and which ones were not. After studying this information, I was able to develop a program to make the trucking operation much more successful. I used the consultant we had hired since we were under contract to pay for the consultant's services whether we used him or not. Why not plug into the numerous opportunities available to help you in your job or organization? These people and services are available to you, but you must take the necessary time to determine if they can help you and then ask for this help.

Another way to add hours to your day is to keep abreast of the latest publications being developed to help you. How do you get information to make your jobs easier and more efficient? One way is to keep a sharp eye on new and emerging sources of information such as directories listing various information all in one source. You might be able to get the information in three or four different places, but it is better to get it in one source. For example, one well-known directory is developed so that the readers of this directory can use it as a promotion mailing list, as a prospect calling list for the sales force, as an executive checklist, or as a buyer's guide. Certain newsletters will give you information about new publications and directories to help you. A recent newsletter made reference to a new manual recently produced by the federal government about services and loans for small businesses in the United States.

Tremendous amounts of material produced by the federal government are produced at nominal cost. Many pamphlets, reports, and manuals are given away free of charge. In the next few pages

I will discuss the information that is available to you free or almost free from the government.

*Using free information.* One of the most common complaints of business people is the high cost of taxes. Statistics show that most people spend the first *five* months of the year paying local, state, and federal taxes. Your taxes pay for a number of services. One of the services performed by the state and federal government is the publication of a number of important reports, folios, books, and so forth.

Each day Washington is turning out new rules and regulations. To keep up with these changes you can read the free government publications explaining these new regulations. Let's look at some of these publications. Many of them can help you.

*A basic guide to exporting.* The U.S. Department of Commerce puts out a booklet on *exporting* which includes information on getting started, selecting sales channels, pricing, financing exports, shipping your products, and promoting your product sales overseas. This sixty-one-page booklet can be obtained by writing to:

Superintendent of Documents
U.S. Government Printing Office
Washington, D.C. 20402

*Car Pool Kit.* To help ease the energy crisis the federal government has become involved with the need to organize and support car pools. The U.S. Department of Transportation has printed up an attractive blue car-pool kit which includes information on the need to car pool, car pools and the employer, car-pool matching approaches, car pools and the community, car pools and the insurance questions, double-up film information, Federal Highway Administration information, and other facts and figures. This kit could be an excellent aid to the individual or department in your company that is concerned with car-pooling. This excellent *free* kit can be obtained by writing:

Double-Up
U.S. Department of Transportation
(HHP-26)
Washington, D.C. 20590


*Energy Conservation Handbook.* Recent studies show that 20 percent to 50 percent of the fuel used by industry is used for plant heating. We need to improve the efficiency of fuel utilization. The U.S. Department of Commerce has recently published the "Energy Conservation Handbook" especially designed for light industries and commercial building. This handbook covers important areas such as the need for additional insulation for many industrial furnaces, wall and roof insulation, heat loss by windows and doors, air conditioning, heating systems, and lighting. This handbook is unique because it lists ways to successfully conserve heat loss, such as by adding insulating glass or weather stripping, avoiding overheating, cleaning filters on air conditioners, replacing lighting with more efficient lamps, and so on. It goes on to indicate who can help, such as the plant engineer, plant manager, plant employees, or maintenance people. You will even get the savings breakdown if you take the steps suggested in this worthwhile handbook. The cost for this publication is only 35 cents and you may get it by writing to:


Energy Conservation Handbook
U.S. Superintendent of Documents
U.S. Government Printing Office
Washington, D.C. 20402


The federal government is doing extensive research and development in the area of energy, but for any energy program to work effectively every worker, consumer, employer, and homeowner must do his or her part to conserve energy and use basic common sense to make the most of our energy.

*Consumer Publications.* Conserving energy is just as essential as conserving our money in making our consumer purchases. The federal government acquires a vast amount of information on products, services, and other subjects of consumer concern. A recently-built publication center has been set up in Pueblo, Colorado, to share the consumer information with the public. The center publishes booklets on consumer subjects such as automobiles, employment, education, food purchasing and preparation, diet and nutrition, health and medicine, recreation, money management, retirement, and landscaping. There are many helpful publications for older Americans.

The consumer booklets cover important subjects such as buying your home or successfully protecting your housing investment. Other important topics include how to choose a vocational school, how to use credit wisely, and what truth in lending means to you.

*How to order these consumer booklets.* Many of the booklets are completely free and some can be purchased for a very small amount. Since there are too many booklets to list, I recommend that you request the current consumer catalog from the following address:

Consumer Information Center
Pueblo, Colorado 81009

The catalog will list all booklets by subject and make it easy for you to order more than one booklet at one time. The information center also welcomes your comments, recommendations, and suggestions for future publications. Take advantage of the excellent publications available to you on consumer information.

*Publications of the Women's Bureau.* The U.S. Department of Labor has developed and published a number of free publications on career opportunities, education and training, child care services, standards and legislation affecting women, and many reports on the status of women in today's work force.

Women have always played a very important role in business and industry. Because of both the high cost of living and the many modern appliances which save the American woman a great deal of time, more women are joining the work force every year.

*How to order Women's Bureau Publications.* To obtain a listing of women's publications, request leaflet number ten from:

Women's Bureau
Employment Standards Administration
U.S. Department of Labor
Washington, D.C. 20210

If you would like to receive notices of future Women's Bureau publications, write to the same address as above. Please state the specific subject in which you are interested and give your name and mailing address.

*Small Business Administration Publications.* The U.S. Small Business Administration annually publishes thousands of booklets to aid the small-business person. The subjects are numerous and far-ranging—from personal selling to accounting, business law, retailing, manufacturing, and budgeting. Many of the publications are offered free of charge, and some of the publications are offered at a nominal price.

You may order your catalog of small-business publications from:

U.S. Small Business Administration
Washington, D.C. 20416

*Trade Associations and Organizations.* Many trade associations produce books, articles, booklets, and other information material that can provide excellent information. You may get the addresses and the name of the association officers in the *Encyclopedia of Associations,* published by Gale Research Company, at your local library.

Associations and trade organizations are very happy to tell you about the latest changes in their particular fields. Write to the associations that are of interest to you and your business and simply ask them to put your name on their mailing lists.

*Schools and Colleges are information centers.* Many schools and colleges spend great sums of money in research and development. Business and industry should make an attempt to use this information. The academic circles can offer many new ideas, but it's up to the business people to evaluate these ideas and determine whether or not they can be used in their businesses. It's a good idea to get your name on the mailing list of a school or a college that is doing research or development in a field that interests you.

*Good information saves your time and money.* Far too many companies hire extra people and spend large sums of time and money doing surveys and research projects that were done in the past. One research manager of a large service company in Boston continually asks himself, "Did we complete a project like this last year?"

If the project was done in the past you may want to use some of that information. If you feel that the research was done years ago, you may find that an updated research project is required to keep your results relevant and timely.

*Problems with too much information.* You may find that in your business you have too much information and that too much of your time is being spent wading in and out of the information. To correct this situation order *only* the information you need and carefully dispose of all unnecessary information and paperwork.

Every company has people who like to send away for free information. Once the information is received it is filed away, never to be used again. Keep in mind both the quality and quantity of your information. Order only information that you feel is relevant to you or your business.

Besides using information, another way to add hours to your day is to concentrate on the "80/20" formula. This formula is used in sales to indicate that 20 percent of the customers will buy 80 percent of the total goods or services sold. Just as the salesperson must concentrate his or her activities on the important 20 percent to attain the important results, you must continue to evaluate your activities to determine whether or not they will give you the results you want to achieve. I have one client who spends a tremendous amount of time and energy complaining about why he cannot do certain jobs and why everything is so much easier for others and so difficult for him. Do you see the difficulties clearer than the opportunities? By getting involved in the important activities you will build confidence in yourself and that confidence will help build a better you. You must make the effort before you can receive the reward. Too many people expect that they can do the minimum and rewards will still arrive for them. The effort must be exerted first. A very successful sales manager uses a prop for all of his sales promotion meetings with his salespeople. The prop—a water pump with a large handle—illustrates his point that the effort must come before the reward. You must pump the handle on a steady basis, over and over again, until the water comes out as the reward. In your management of time, you must pump your effort into your work often enough and long enough and with the sufficient force before you can get the reward. Use your time to attain the important results you want to achieve.

In essence, you can add hours to your normal day by looking at it in an objective manner. Do you need to follow your normal habits, or can you make some necessary changes to reach your goals? Life management is being able to discipline yourself to do the necessary jobs at the right time. You can add hours by watching out for your natural inclination to procrastinate. The Iranian hostage added hours to his normal day by saying "no" to his friend who wanted to play cards all day. Instead, he spent the morning reading his books. By keeping all your notes, appointments, and other information in one book, you will be able to add hours to your day. Use new ideas to do hard work the easy way. Use the latest information to make your job easier. Use the government's numerous publications and aids. Take a careful look at how you spend your time, and then take the necessary steps to add hours to your normal work day.

*Conclusion.* Many people complain loudly and often about their workload but few people do anything about it. It's a good idea to look closely at your workload to find out what's on it and how long it will take to complete the major and minor items. You will be able to cut your workload and still accomplish MORE if you consider the following time-saving ideas:

1. Try to get out of some of your work. With the extra time you might be able to use it to think and plan for your company.
2. Are you taking on too many assignments yourself? Take some time to decide on which people in your office can handle these assignments.
3. Learn to delegate assignments; after delegating an assignment, stay close enough to the work so you can answer questions and know when the job is completed.
4. Even if the people in your department seem very busy, be certain you know what they are doing. They may be doing unnecessary or low-priority work when they could very well be doing top-priority work for the company.
5. Try to get your employees to do their jobs completely. Permit them to take their own responsibility. You will make your workers grow if you demand that they perform better work.
6. Make a list of the most important items you want to accomplish each day. This excellent guide helps you stay on top of the high-priority items and, most importantly, helps you complete them.
7. Paperwork can be a great time waster and accounts for a large part of your workload. Try to handle each piece of paper once. If you cannot use it throw it away. Update your files as often as necessary and throw away all unnecessary papers.
8. Use your commuting time to your advantage. A major train company set up special cars to offer business- and college-

level courses for their commuters. The program is now so successful that both undergraduate and graduate courses are offered.

Only you can manage your time. It's not an easy job, but the rewards are enormous. You will be able to do other important work that was long neglected because of your gigantic workload.

# 16
# HOW TO MAKE
# YOUR TIME PAY

The end of the day is an excellent time to examine the achievement of goals or the lack thereof. Here are some comments very typical of people trying to manage their time in the world of work:

- "It was such a busy day I simply forgot the deadline."
- "I only wish I could spend the necessary time on the ABC Company account."
- "I'll never get through all the work. I'll probably come in on Saturday."
- "My highest-, top-level-priority job was delayed because I spent a good part of my day helping my assistant."
- "I'm dead tired. I know I try to do too much myself, but nobody else can do it."
- "I started the day with a couple of jobs I felt were quick, easy jobs, but they consumed the full day."
- "Yes, I spent the full morning on paperwork, but I wanted to be sure the work was right."
- "How can I get my work done? The main office wants all these reports done for them."
- "Yes, I know how important the Adex Project will be for the company, but I still need the preliminary research to start it."

- "Yes, I find myself doing routine work, but the company will not hire other people to help me."
- "I try to do one thing at a time, and I seem to get further and further behind in my work."
- "My job keeps me so busy, I know I waste some time doing some things I should not do. But how do I know which activities I should stop right now?"
- "I know I waste time, but I feel that I'm doing many things in my job that are not on my job description."
- "I know I'm spending a lot of my time on the phone because my time log shows over two hours each day. I would like to cut down."

People are full of very logical and sincere rationalizations to defend their lack of real accomplishments in day-to-day battles with the hour glass. Why? Simply because of a real lack of self-management, and a disability to zero in on the real reasons why time is winning the battle. Let's take each comment above and make some constructive suggestions to help win the battle for your most important resource—your TIME.

"*It was such a busy day I simply forgot the deadline.*" Far too many people fail to really manage their time and permit the work load in their office or company to dictate their own actions. There are many jobs and assignments that can take your time: filing, writing letters, phone calls, reading memorandums, double checking on assignments and jobs requiring no additional checking, and many others. Many successful time managers make a list of the priorities they want to accomplish during that day. Your top priority can be started early in the day so you can tackle it with your full energy. The lower-priority jobs can be handled later in the day when your energy level is lower because you used your top energy to do the most important jobs. In every office, a percentage of the workers are very busy, but the most important work is being done by the people who are not only working hard, but intelligently as well. Everyone can miss a deadline once in a while, but missing too many deadlines might indicate a real need to plan your day's work segments so that you get the most important work done on time.

"*I only wish I could spend the necessary time on the ABC Company account.*" How important is the ABC Company account to you? Will this account give you the sales and profits your company needs? Do you spend too much time talking about it and never get around to working on it? Can you delegate some of the preliminary work on the ABC Company to one of your assistants? Good time managers have the ability to act on their ideas. If they feel that a certain job should be completed, they set the necessary plans into action so that the job can be completed. Do you wait until tomorrow to do things? If you wait an extra day or extra week, the competition can gain the extra edge they need to beat you to the punch. Everyone knows the story of the inventor who finished half of one product and put it aside to work on when he found the time. Then someone else's version of the product came out on the market and sold in the millions. When you determine the job or assignment has merit, put it on your list of "things to do" or delegate it to someone to get it done for you.

"*I'll never get through all this work. I'll probably come in on Saturday.*" The most important question you must ask yourself in order to handle this problem of too much work is simply: *why* is the work coming to you? Why are you so overloaded with work? Do you take the necessary time to weed out the trivial work from the work that is "high payoff"? "High payoff" work is that which will give you the best return on investment for your time. In your job you are being paid for your time and your ability to perform at a maximum level to accomplish certain jobs, so those jobs should be important or "high payoff" jobs. Look around the office. Do you see any other people managing their time successfully and keeping their workload down to a minimum? One very successful time manager found herself coming into work on Saturdays and Sundays to keep up with the huge workload. She decided to use a formula called the Four D's of Time Management: quickly *d*rop the unimportant; *d*elay the less important work; *d*elegate the routine jobs; and *d*o the "high payoff" work—not necessarily all by herself, but getting others in her office to help lighten her load for the good of the whole company or organization. Many successful people find that by getting other people behind their ideas and assignments more work can be completed. Are you getting work that could be handled by others? As long as you continue to do the work yourself, the work will continue to come to you. Only you can make the necessary changes to cut your own workload and enjoy your weekends.

"*My highest-, top-level-priority job was delayed because I spent a good part of the day helping my assistant.*" Why did you hire your assistant? I'm sure you hired your assistant to help you accomplish more and higher-priority work. Since you didn't mention that your assistant is in a training process, I cannot see why you lose all that precious time in a helping situation. Are your assistants qualified to handle their work? Everyone puts a certain degree of importance on various tasks on his job. In some cases people tend to overestimate the importance of work and the real priority of some tasks. Many very capable assistants steal valuable time and effort from their bosses by asking them to help do work the assistants were hired to perform. I was in the office of a manager of a large industrial account when his assistant came in and asked him for help picking up a display for a photography session the following day. The manager replied, "To be quite frank, Joe, I would rather not be a furniture mover." Here is a case where an assistant became a burden rather than an assistant.[1]

The way an assistant performs depends to a large extent on how the manager communicates this important message: You can handle your job, just keep me posted on the important subjects. I hired you to make an important contribution to the company. Millions of hours are spent in the world of work by assistants and bosses spending time doing the routine and unimportant work. One assistant manager in Massachusetts saved much time of his own by simply asking his boss to give him a list of the most important work he wanted on a weekly or monthly basis. A good assistant can

1. William J. Bond, "Secrets To Success In Your Job," Career Publishing, Haverhill, Massachusetts, p. 63.

relieve the boss of much detail work in many ways, even by going so far as to organize his thoughts for him.[2]

Your assistants must aid you in the accomplishment of your top priorities—not delay them. Only you can manage your assistants to run the team successfully.

"*I'm dead tired. I know I try to do too much myself, but nobody else can do it.*" In each and every office we find at least one person who feels that he or she possesses such super talents and abilities that no one else can handle the work. This same attitude is the reason that so many very high-salaried executives and managers find themselves doing work that could very well be delegated to others. This style of work is not only detrimental for the worker, but it's costly for the company. A good time manager knows that he or she must encourage growth within the company to permit others to learn and grow into newer and more important responsibilities. People within the organization who keep the work to themselves will stifle the others.

This comment is very common for supervisors in the world of work. The job of supervising is a very difficult one. It becomes even more difficult when the supervisor or manager takes on too many jobs that should be delegated to his or her assistants to help them learn more about the supervisor's job. One supervisor found that he was spending almost 80 percent of his total work day doing work that could very well be handled by others. He decided to turn more and more of his routine work over to his assistants, and found them eager and competent to do this work. He also found a great deal more time to do just what he was hired to do: supervise his department.

"*I started the day with a couple of jobs I felt were quick, easy jobs, but they consumed the full day.*" The biggest time killers in the working world can be the easy or quick jobs. Too many of the easy or quick jobs are started early in the day and stretch out to the greater part of the day. One of the biggest disadvantages of going to work on these quick jobs is that they consume not only

2. *Harvard Business Review*, p. 209, July 1979.

your precious time but your energy as well. I had a young lady at a recent time-management seminar who claimed that, in setting up her priorities for the next day, she would always put on the top of the list of "things to do" the easy and quick jobs. She found that she never got to the highly important jobs because of this desire to get the quick, routine, and so-called faster jobs out of the way. Is it possible to find someone else in your office to handle the routine and quick jobs for you? Can you delay the routine jobs until you have finished the more important jobs? One very successful time manager in Georgia has a system to avoid handling the low-priority jobs. Each morning he separates his work into three categories. One stack of work is labeled *low*-priority work, another stack is *medium*-priority work, and the third stack is the *top*-priority work. His general rule is that he will not permit himself to do any low-priority work as long as he has a stack of medium- or high-priority items. He first tackles the high-priority stack and determines which is the "high-payoff" job in this stack and starts to work on this job. In many cases he will work on this job until he goes home at night. During the day he delegates work out of his medium-priority stack to his assistants. Once the medium-priority items are completed he then delegates the low-priority work. This system gives him an opportunity to do the high-priority work and get help on the other work as well.

"*Yes, I spent the full morning on paperwork, but I wanted to be sure it was done right.*" This comment was made at a question-and-answer period when I spoke at a national sales meeting. This salesman claimed he spent his valuable time each morning doing the routine paperwork. Successful time managers have a very important skill that is developed after working in a job for a certain time. This skill is a TIME-MANAGEMENT CONSCIOUSNESS—a real understanding of the true value of time—which never permits time wasters like routine paperwork to take away the most valuable time during the day. Good time managers make certain that a job is done the easy way and not with time-consuming, difficult, outdated methods. A good time manager may not be the most popular person in the office, but he has the ability to say "NO" to people within the office or company who try to steal his time with "low payoff" jobs. I overheard one very successful time manager say to another worker over the phone, "Sorry, I cannot answer that question. I promised you that information next week. Please avoid calling me until I can develop that information." This is a good example of saying "*NO*" and meaning it. As long as you permit others to steal your valuable time for low-priority items, your high-priority items will be buried in your box.

"*How can I get my work done? The main office wants all these reports done for them.*" It's easy and sometimes good to complain and let out some steam about your job. Each job has certain characteristics that make you feel like you are being stretched in many different directions. In order to get back on the right track you must ask yourself some valuable questions. Why is the main office asking you to do the reports? Can someone else in your office help you with the reports or can you delegate some of the work to others? What work has the highest priority—the work for the main office, or the work in your own office? Ask the main office if you can hire someone to help you accomplish these extra reports. You might find that the main office will cut back their requests for these reports when they realize that additional people must be hired to complete the work. Let the main office know that your current work is being neglected because you want to finish their work. Why take all these responsibilities on yourself? The work will increase and increase unless you let your boss know about this situation. One of the problems with too many irons in the fire is that eventually the fire goes out.

"*Yes, I know how important the Adex Project will be for the company, but I still need the preliminary research to start it.*" We can very easily put off a number one priority because we want to get other work completed to make the job easier to start. This is similar to the writer waiting for his electric typewriter to come back from the service shop when he has a manual typewriter that works just as well. Why not start the Adex Project without the preliminary research? Once the job is started, you may find that the preliminary steps are not required or that only certain preliminary steps are needed. Some people want to find excuses just to delay a difficult or not-too-popular job. One manager, Claire U., needed an advertising specialist in her office to help with the growing sales force and increasing sales of the business. She delayed advertising for the position because she waited first for the boss to determine the pay scale for this new job. The hiring was further delayed because a new office was needed for this new employee. Weeks flew by, then months. The employee was never hired and new priorities came on the scene. The delay hurt the manager and the company. By delaying the important work, you might lose out on an important employee, idea, or method that would help you progress in your job even better. If you feel that a certain job is needed, a new machine is needed, or a new method is needed, avoid the reaction to put it off; do it now. Reap the benefits of your decision later.

   "*Yes, I find myself doing routine work, but the company will not hire other people to help me.*" How much is your time really worth? How much is an hour worth? Ten dollars? Twenty-four dollars? Fifty dollars? One hundred dollars? Five hundred dollars? One time manager will ask himself this question to get himself on the right track: "Where should I spend my time right this very minute?" Routine work consumes your time just as fast as the "high-payoff" work. I was amazed to see some very highly-paid executives doing their own filing at a time when the secretary was without work. This problem also arises at home during your leisure time. For example, one morning recently I drove along the main road near home. I passed a disabled car. Its driver was working on the car to get it going again. I rode by about four hours later and the same man was still working on that car. How much is his time worth? The mechanic at the nearby garage might be able to fix it within one hour. Why try to become a mechanic and spend all that valuable time when you could turn the work over to a specialist? Use your time in the most valuable way possible. Why spend fifty dollars in energy for a ten dollar job? You must be aware of your talents and what things you should be doing to make the best use of your time. One time manager uses a form on her desk that she looks at each day before filling her "to do" list:

- Maybe I don't need to _____ anymore.
- Perhaps I need to _____ now.
- I want to delegate _____ today.

You must develop a real money and time consciousness in order to utilize your time successfully. At home or at the office, you must take a hard look at your work and your time value. Why spend all day fixing your car or doing the routine work yourself, when you can hire someone to do it faster and better than you? You can then spend your time in the "high-payoff" work. It will take time to develop your time consciousness but it will pay off for you in the future.

*"I try to do one thing at a time, and I seem to get further and further behind in my work."* In this book I have talked about doing the most important priority first and staying on that priority until you have finished it. In many cases you must use your time even more efficiently to get the maximum results. For example, you're on the phone, and for one reason or another there is a delay. Your party is coming to the phone, or getting some additional information for you. Use that waiting time properly. Why not read over the communication pertinent to the conversation you are about to have on the phone? Other good time managers will add up a column of figures on the calculator, or straighten out a series of papers on a particular subject. Make the best of this waiting time. One left-handed office worker found that she could run a business machine with her right hand while writing information with her left hand. Do you try to do more than one thing at a time?

As a writer I try to observe people, especially the way they manage their time. Time management is really life management. Last week I was taking a coffee break in a coffee shop. One young lady came into the shop with a baby a few months old and another toddler about two years old. She ordered something while holding the baby. Then, while eating with one hand, she fed the baby with the other hand. Once the baby was fed, she continued to eat her own food, and started to look over her checkbook to determine the cash balance. She made some notations in the checkbook and then started to think about something. She next lit a

cigarette and conversed with the other youngster with her. Then she
checked the baby's diaper and went back to her meal. This is an
excellent example of using your time to the fullest—getting it all
together to reach your success. Just as this parent must utilize all her
skills to do her job, in the world of work the supervisor must do the
same to reach his or her goals at work. In a recent study of
supervisors searching for their day-to-day activities, I found that
they averaged 583 activities per each eight-hour shift—an average of
one every forty-eight seconds. In order for these supervisors to
succeed, they must be able to handle many activities at the same
time. You must also watch out for the many smaller, unimportant
items which can steal your valuable time. Your time is money.

*"My job keeps me so busy, I know I waste some time doing
some things I should not do. But how do I know which activities I
should stop right now?"* What is causing the most time-consumption?
What is an average day's work? Do you spend a large part of your
day on the phone? Would you say that all that time is necessary on
the phone? Can you cut some of that phone time? How much time is
being spent on the routine jobs? Do you see too many visitors in
your company? How much time is spent doing this? Can someone
else see those visitors? Do you spend a great deal of your time
answering simple questions? Do you train your people well enough
so they can handle problems for themselves? Or do you set things up
so that questions will be coming to you? One executive of a large oil
company found that he was spending more and more work time
handling work that he knew he should delegate to others. But he
was unwilling to "dump memory," or tell what he knew about a
particular job or project, because he felt that it would take too long.
Therefore he took the projects on himself. In order to determine
how much time you're presently using that is wasteful to you and
your organization, you need to run a check on yourself. Your time is
money. Do you ever waste money? There's a good possibility that
you take every precaution to watch your money, so why not run a
check on the way you spend an average day? On Page 150 you will
find a time log to fill in the activities of your average day. What is the
task? What is the priority number? Is it your number one priority?

Number two or three? What are the comments on your use of time? You will find using the time log will help you stop the numerous leaks in your own time-management program. Notice every time sequence is fifteen minutes. A number of jobs and tasks can be accomplished in this short period of time. Just as the average supervisor completes an activity each forty-eight seconds, a large number of jobs can be accomplished in a short period of time. Examine each minute of your time, and determine how you are presently spending it. The "task" simply means the particular activity you did at that time. Did you write a report, or spend time on the phone during the period from 9:00 to 9:15 in the morning? List your activities for the full day; this will give you an excellent idea of your normal day. The priority number will be from one to three. The number one priority will be a "high-payoff" activity, one that must be completed for you to be successful in your job or in your goals. A number one priority for your time at home might be to spend more time with your hobbies, more time in your MY time. A salesperson might find priority number one will be getting appointments to present his or her new sales presentation.

The number two priority is of average importance and therefore must be classified as such. For the person at home, this priority might be the routine house or yard work that must be completed, but does not have the "payoff" for the time invested that the number one priority has. A salesperson might classify routine letters as a number two priority, or the paperwork for sales meetings as a number two priority. The number two priorities have some importance to you and the organization, but are not the top priorities and therefore should not be given your best time such as early in the morning, or your prime time when you're at your peak of efficiency.

The number three priority is work that should be classified as "no-no" work. This work is not essential to your success, and can be completed by someone else or stopped right away. Examples of number threes are filing, making excessive personal telephone calls during prime time, setting up personal engagements during prime time, duplicating effort, socializing, performing menial tasks, attending pointless meetings, or any other tasks that are not essential

Date _____ Name _____

| TIME | TASK | PRIORITY NUMBER | COMMENTS ON EFFECTIVE USE OF TIME |
|---|---|---|---|
| 9:00 – 9:15 | | | |
| 9:15 – 9:30 | | | |
| 9:30 – 9:45 | | | |
| 9:45 – 10:00 | | | |
| 10:00 – 10:15 | | | |
| 10:15 – 10:30 | | | |
| 10:30 – 10:45 | | | |
| 10:45 – 11:00 | | | |
| 11:00 – 11:15 | | | |
| 11:15 – 11:30 | | | |
| 11:30 – 11:45 | | | |
| 11:45 – 12:00 | | | |
| 12:00 – 12:15 | | | |
| 12:15 – 12:30 | | | |
| 12:30 – 12:45 | | | |
| 12:45 – 1:00 | | | |
| 1:00 – 1:15 | | | |
| 1:15 – 1:30 | | | |
| 1:30 – 1:45 | | | |
| 1:45 – 2:00 | | | |
| 2:00 – 2:15 | | | |
| 2:15 – 2:30 | | | |
| 2:30 – 2:45 | | | |
| 2:45 – 3:00 | | | |
| 3:00 – 3:15 | | | |
| 3:15 – 3:30 | | | |
| 3:30 – 3:45 | | | |
| 3:45 – 4:00 | | | |
| 4:00 – 4:15 | | | |
| 4:15 – 4:30 | | | |
| 4:30 – 4:45 | | | |
| 4:45 – 5:00 | | | |

General Review and Comments _____

_____

_____

Grade _____

**ILLUSTRATION 11.**

to you. If you find that there seems to be a trend of number threes that are consuming your time, this important log will indicate this to you.

The last section of the time log is the comments section. In this section you should indicate your reaction to your time use. Why did you spend fifteen minutes filing? Did you accomplish anything in that staff meeting? Why did you accept those four routine telephone calls in your prime time periods? This section is very important because it gives you an opportunity to fully evaluate the use of your time. Once you see a trend of accepting too many telephone calls that are of less than real importance, you might use the "call back" method whereby you take the individual's telephone number and call him or her back at your convenience. Be selfish with your time. The time log will help you become even more selfish and more effective in your use of your time.

How do you use the time log? Try it for at least one week. You can easily make additional time log sheets for this purpose. During your normal workday fill in the task for each fifteen-minute segment. You should be concerned primarily with recording as accurately as possible the different tasks and the approximate time spent on each one. At the end of each day, fill in the priority number for each task. Was it a number one? A number two or three? Now make your own comments on the use of time. Was it a waste of time for you? Why or why not? Write down just what you think; no one will see this time log but you. Writing down your own personal comments will help you identify both the number threes and your reactions. Notice on Illustration 12 on Page 153 how this time manager showed that the phone calls and filing were real time wasters. He mentioned that he did the filing because he was avoiding the number one priority of doing the report for the ABC Company. Also on Illustration 12 on the bottom of the page you will find a *General Review and Comments* section. This is a general statement for the day, and in this section you can grade yourself for the day on your time management. How did you mind your time today? A? A-? B? B-? C? C-? This grade will give you the motivation to go to the next day and beat your record. Keep trying to get your grade up to A. If you find that you're able to give yourself an A, good; keep it there. You may want to give this time log a check again six months from now. If you get a different job or a promotion, you might want to give yourself a time log check to determine if you are spending your time in the "high payoff" work.

"*I know I waste time, but I feel that I'm doing many things in my job that are not on my job description.*" This is a common occurrence, especially in a company growing so rapidly it fails to keep up with the numerous new jobs. The best way to handle this situation is to take a close look at your job description. What does your job description include?

After checking your job description check it with your time log. What items that are high or low priorities in your time log are not included in your job description? If you find many jobs and tasks are not included in your job description, it's time to talk to your boss or your supervisor about this. Are you doing two or three jobs? Did your job change or increase because of additional business? Did you pick up additional jobs because some people left the company and replacements were never hired? One supervisor of a small company found himself trying to do three different jobs, because the company never hired new people once employees left the company. The sales grew and the workforce got smaller, resulting in too much work for some employees. It's a good idea to look over the job description on a regular basis to be sure you're doing the job the company expects you to do.

"*I know I'm spending a lot of my time on the phone because my time log shows over two hours each day. I would like to cut down.*" The telephone can be one of the most valuable tools to save time. On the other hand it could also be one of the largest time robbers in your office or at home. You mentioned that you spent two hours on the phone, but you didn't discuss the importance of the calls. Some occupations require spending a large part of the work day on the phone. Salespeople must use the phone to make appointments and to discuss service problems with their customers. Stockbrokers spend a large amount of their time on the phone. Recent studies of

Date __March 1__     Name __E. Rosenfeld__

| TIME | TASK | PRIORITY NUMBER | COMMENTS ON EFFECTIVE USE OF TIME |
|------|------|-----------------|-----------------------------------|
| 9:00 – 9:15 | Reading Mail | 3 | Poor Use of Time |
| 9:15 – 9:30 | " | 3 | " |
| 9:30 – 9:45 | Five-Year Plan | 1 | Excellent |
| 9:45 – 10:00 | " | 1 | " |
| 10:00 – 10:15 | " | 1 | " |
| 10:15 – 10:30 | " | 1 | " |
| 10:30 – 10:45 | " | 1 | " |
| 10:45 – 11:00 | Coffee | | |
| 11:00 – 11:15 | Five-Year Plan | 1 | |
| 11:15 – 11:30 | " | 1 | |
| 11:30 – 11:45 | " | 1 | |
| 11:45 – 12:00 | " | 1 | I'm proud |
| 12:00 – 12:15 | " | 1 | of myself |
| 12:15 – 12:30 | " | 1 | |
| 12:30 – 12:45 | Lunch | | |
| 12:45 – 1:00 | " | | |
| 1:00 – 1:15 | " | | |
| 1:15 – 1:30 | " | | |
| 1:30 – 1:45 | Phone | 3 | Avoiding 5-yr. plan |
| 1:45 – 2:00 | Reading Memos | 3 | " |
| 2:00 – 2:15 | Filing | 3 | " |
| 2:15 – 2:30 | Filing | 3 | " |
| 2:30 – 2:45 | Five-Year Plan | 1 | Essential Work |
| 2:45 – 3:00 | " | 1 | " |
| 3:00 – 3:15 | " | 1 | " |
| 3:15 – 3:30 | " | 1 | " |
| 3:30 – 3:45 | " | 1 | " |
| 3:45 – 4:00 | Break | 2 | |
| 4:00 – 4:15 | Filing Memos | 3 | Needed to clear desk |
| 4:15 – 4:30 | Write letter | 2 | Need a break from |
| 4:30 – 4:45 | " | 2 | Five-Year Plan |
| 4:45 – 5:00 | " | 2 | " |

General Review and Comments     Spent too much time on reading and opening mail.
I need to cut filing to a minimum. I'm happy with my ability to stay on five-year plan.

Grade     B+

**ILLUSTRATION 12.**

executives and managers found that they spend on the average at least one hour on the phone. Four out of every ten executives spend over two hours on the phone each day. The major question is whether or not your telephone time is productive or not. Do you spend too much time socializing on the phone? Do you find it difficult to terminate conversations because you feel obligated to continue to speak to the other party? Can you say "goodbye" graciously? Can some of your calls be made at the end of the day, or at the end of the week or even month? One large electronics company found that a great deal of time was spent by employees calling plants in other parts of the country to attain information that would be available in a few days. The information, in report form, was in transit anyway. Why do you need that information today? Why not work on another task or job until that information arrives? Excessive use of the phone is caused by poor telephone habits, and many people use the phone to give the appearance of looking busy. If you're always willing to take your telephone calls promptly, without regard to the priority at hand, you will develop a reputation as a good person to call to get a quick response to questions and problems. Is it possible to get someone to screen your calls? Can you get the caller to call you back at another time? Can you call the caller back at another time? One time manager from Massachusetts finds he saves time by making all of his calls the first thing in the morning. He finds that it's much easier to reach people first thing in the morning. In the past he had called people during the prime time hours at work from 10 A.M. to 2 P.M. and had found most people were in meetings, out of the office, tied up with customers, or at lunch. You may find that by using the phone at other times besides the prime time you will be much more productive with the telephone.

How can you cut down on nonproductive use of the phone? One way to accomplish this is to review closely the time log for the length of time you spend on the phone. How much time do you spend each day? Take a look at your time log on Page 150. What are your comments about these telephone calls? Do you go to the phone when you want to avoid a number one priority? Do you use the phone to use up the few minutes before lunch or at the end of your

workday? Do you find that you receive calls that must be trans-
ferred to others in your office or company? Does your secretary or
receptionist know the exact jobs you handle in the company? If your
job description changes frequently, you may want to keep the
telephone operator or receptionist up to date to save you time.
Make sure that your secretary screens all necessary calls for you.

Now you must develop a method to analyze your telephone calls.
One of the best tools available to analyze your telephone time is
the Telephone Call Analysis Card. This card, shown on Page
156, gives you all the relevant information you need for every
call you make or receive. This card system can be used for a two- or
three-week period. The real value of this method is that it gives you
an opportunity to determine if the call could be better handled by a
short memo. The average business telephone call should be just a
few minutes. Longer telephone calls might be handled by a business
letter. Record all calls you make and receive on these cards.

Now the cards can be shuffled in a manner to give you specific
information you need. For example, look at the section in the block
titled: Could someone else have handled? How many of these cards
show that someone else could have handled the call? You're getting
paid too much to handle routine jobs. How many cards indicate that
the call was from Bill Smith, your assistant, located in another building? Perhaps you can limit his calls to one each day at a particular
time, and force him to group his calls, rather than spread them out all
day long. You might want the cards grouped into conversations of over
five minutes. Why do you have calls that last ten and fifteen minutes? A letter or a short memo might be better for you. Do you get
calls on the same subject? One manager in charge of an educational
company started to receive a large amount of calls to reserve space
for their seminars. The manager decided after looking at his telephone analysis cards that these calls should go to someone else in his
office to save his time, and time and money for the company. The
cards can also be an aid in determining for the salesperson how
many sales are made. How often did you speak to the ABC account in
the last two weeks, or month? What companies are calling you about
your product or services? Was the call a follow-up on an advertise-

ment or one of your letters? All this information will aid you in marketing research. On the very bottom of the Telephone Call Analysis Card you will find some space to record other relevant information about the call. How many interruptions did you have during the call? Did the other party leave the phone to get some information from his files? Did you prepare yourself for the call? Did you receive information you already had over the phone? Now that you have the necessary cards and the information you need, take the necessary steps to make better use of your telephone time. If you continue to let the telephone control you, your number one priority will gather dust waiting for you to get to it.

---

### TELEPHONE CALL ANALYSIS CARD

Your name: _____          Date: _____

Person I talked to:          Call initiated by:              Time in
_____            Self _____          Minutes:
Subject: _____            Other Party _____      _____
_____
_____            Could someone else have handled? _____
_____
                             Who? _____

Was call a follow-up of correspondence? _____ of previous call? _____

Would a brief memo have taken less time and served equally

Value of call in relation to my priorities: Low ___ Medium ___ High ___

---

Use this space to record any other pertinent information you wish to study, such as number of interruptions during call. Did you have to wait while your assistant looked up relative information? Etc.

**ILLUSTRATION 13.**

## Summary

Time management, just like any other form of management, requires your full control and direction of your actions. Spending time complaining or rationalizing about why you cannot reach your goals only wastes more time. Use that time to find out new ways to use your time. You are in business for yourself, whether you work for the ABC Company or the XYZ Company. You're selling your skills, talents, and abilities for your salary. You are also selling your ability to use your time successfully to accomplish your goals and objectives. Avoid the routine jobs. Spend your time where it counts on the "high payoff" jobs. Why is all the work coming to you? Avoid overprotecting your assistants. Let your assistants do the work you hired them to do. Watch for the easy or quick jobs that consume your time. Develop a time-management program. Protect yourself so you can accomplish your goals and objectives.

# 17
# WHY LEADERS
# MAKE MORE MONEY
# FOR THEIR TIME

Why do leaders make so much more money than many other people in the world of work? The chairman of the board for one of the largest corporations in the world was asked this question on a recent radio show. The week prior to the show, a business article had detailed the salaries for the top leaders in American business. The caller asked the board chairman, "Sir, just what type of work do you do to deserve the $850,000 salary you receive each year?" The chairman replied, "I work night and day. I deal with tremendous problems. I am forced to make decisions, very difficult decisions, every day. My salary is handled by a separate committee." The chairman makes an important point here. He is being paid this large salary to make important decisions. This man is making that large salary because he decides on major problems. He may not be right in all cases but usually he makes the right choice.

Leaders find that they deal with two basic elements at all times. One is the problem and the other is the decision how to deal with the problem. Good leaders take the necessary time to define and redefine the problem. Let's say, for example, you own a car dealership that sells primarily full-sized cars, and this has always been a very profitable business for you. You notice that in the past few months your customers have been asking about the gas mileage of the new full-sized models, and also about the price and gas mileage of the smaller-sized models. Now, what is the problem? Look at it carefully. All we can see in the beginning are symptoms. The symptoms in this case are the objections to the full-sized cars. As a leader you must try to break through the surface of symptoms to locate the real problem. The real problem may be whether or not more medium- or small-sized cars should be made available at the car dealership. Don't spend too much time trying to find the answer before you have taken time to fully define the problem. If you finally determine that the problem is that car buyers are looking for smaller cars to reduce the cost of running their autos, you are now ready to make your decision.

What will your decision be at this time? Your decision could be to communicate to the manufacturer of your cars that your customers are making numerous requests for information and prices for the smaller automobiles. Now it will be up to the manufacturer to take the information and act on it. You have done your work; you have defined the problem and made the necessary decision. Again, leadership is being able to deal with both the problems and the decisions to solve the problems. Take the necessary time to decide how to tackle important problems.

Good leadership is important for the success of a company or organization. Everyone loves a leader. When people find that you can lead they will follow you. When they find that you cannot lead, they will not follow you—they will move to the new leader. The ancient Greek philosophers worshipped their great leaders, and Plato and Aristotle worked hard to describe the characteristics of the ideal leader. Just what dimensions of personality make a successful leader?

A well-known business writer has developed a listing of twenty dimensions of personality of leaders—from the ability to conceptualize, to organize, to the use of careful judgment, to the physical stamina needed for leadership success. Illustration 14 gives an indication that your adaptability could range from one of having many personal, physical, and family problems, thereby not tolerating stress well; to that of the leader who takes whatever comes down the pike and thrives on it. It would be a very unusual leader who scored high in all dimensions of the leadership personality.

## ILLUSTRATION 14. DIMENSIONS OF LEADERS' PERSONALITIES[1]

| THINKING | Poor | Fair | Good |
|---|---|---|---|
| 1. Capacity to abstract, to conceptualize, to organize, and to integrate different data into a coherent frame of reference. | Thinks concretely, item by item, fact by fact. | Can relate theory to management problems, but doesn't search out concepts and ideas. | Encyclopedic synthesist, able to organize and integrate creatively principles, values, concepts, and information from full range of arts and sciences. |
| 2. Tolerance for ambiguity, can stand confusion until things become clear. | Needs to keep focus on one defined project at a time. | Can handle vague project guidelines, but must always be anchored to concrete structure or method. | Can tolerate ambiguity for years, doesn't get anxious waiting for long-term plans to come to fruition. |
| 3. Intelligence, has the capacity not only to abstract, but also to be practical. | Educated, but not very imaginative or creative. | Bright, makes good use of experience. Sometimes might seem like a hustler. | Exceptionally bright, draws on a fountain of experience. Good street smarts. |
| 4. Judgment, knows when to act. | Rushes to judgment, without thinking things through. | Thoughtful, but never quite sees the whole picture of implications. | Excellent judgment, very few mistakes over the years. |
| **FEELINGS AND INTERRELATIONS** | | | |
| 5. Authority, has the feeling that he or she belongs in boss's role. | Bends over backward to please; can't give direction or control. | Doesn't apologize for being boss, but feels arrived at position by luck and is thus tentative. | A "natural" in position. Takes full charge. Reasonably certain will do it well and probably better than most. |

*(Continued)*

**ILLUSTRATION 14. (Continued)**

| FEELINGS AND INTERRELATIONS | Poor | Fair | Good |
|---|---|---|---|
| 6. Activity, takes a vigorous orientation to problems and needs of the organization. | Reactive, moves when prodded. Often does not want to know information. | Attacks problems in fairly secure arenas, but takes little risk. Subordinates feel "not going any place." | Attacks problems strategically, with well-defined targets. Plans long-term, step-by-step inexorable advance ahead of competition. |
| 7. Achievement, oriented toward organization's success rather than personal aggrandizement. | Wants to achieve, but passions don't match competence. | Intense wish to achieve that overflows into full effort, but competes too harshly and abrasively. May be ruthless. Strong need to control others. | Very motivated to move upward as recognition of competence. May be disappointed if not chosen but not hungry for applause. Organization's achievements are seen as personal achievements. |
| 8. Sensitivity, able to perceive subtleties of others' feelings. | Obtuse, can't read people's faces or their feelings between the lines of what they say. | Picks up feelings and reads body movements, but sometimes too glibly, which may result in seeing feelings as superficial and manipulatable. | Master at sensing feelings, anticipating them, and taking them seriously. |

| | | |
|---|---|---|
| 9. Involvement, sees oneself as a participating member of an organization. | Never leaves desk, won't go into the field. | Gets out sporadically, reluctantly, and perfunctorily, and doesn't learn much. | Allocates serious, continuing time to field visits. Mixes with employees, seeking information on their problems. Summarizes findings for employees and managers. Has finger on the pulse of the organization. |
| 10. Maturity, has good relationships with authority figures. | Still an adolescent, always challenging bosses and resisting authority. | Hard to predict. Sometimes has easy relationships, sometimes uncomfortable, depending on kind of boss. | Works well with authority figures. Uniformly praised by all bosses for smoothness of working relationships with them. |
| 11. Interdependence, accepts appropriate dependency needs of others as well as of him or herself. | Needs continuous direction and well-defined structure. | Insists on standing alone and denies need for others. | Stands on own but invites information, criticism, and cooperation from others. Can yield temporarily to lead of more competent, person without feeling loss of leadership role. |
| 12. Articulateness, makes a good impression. | Clearly upset even when presenting reports in small meetings. | Can make a decent presentation but it's hard work. Doesn't read audience well, seems somehow removed. | Extremely presentable, has a wide-ranging vocabulary. Inspires audience confidence, senses audience moods. Respected by peers for verbalizing and presenting their problems. |

*(Continued)*

163

**ILLUSTRATION 14. (Continued)**

| FEELINGS AND INTERRELATIONS | Poor | Fair | Good |
|---|---|---|---|
| 13. Stamina, has physical as well as mental energy. | Low level of involvement and enthusiasm, so runs down fast. | Can work through a significant problem at good energy level. | Consistent high energy level. Always at the ready. Doesn't seem to run out of steam, paces him or herself well. |
| 14. Adaptability, manages stress well. | Doesn't tolerate stress well. Many physical, personal, and family symptoms. | Does reasonably well under bursts of stress but not long, sustained pressures. Worries in a healthy way about solutions to problems. | Takes whatever comes down the pike and seems to thrive on it. |
| 15. Sense of humor, doesn't take self too seriously. | Can't laugh at anything. Somber, forbidding, cold. | Laughs too easily at everything. Sometimes laughs inappropriately to ease own tension. Immature raconteur. | Warm affectionate humor. Stories appropriate to place and position. Eases tensions naturally. Is welcome company. |
| **OUTWARD BEHAVIOR CHARACTERISTICS** | | | |
| 16. Vision, is clear about progression of his or her own life and career, as well as where the organization would go. | Takes no interest in career, content to move along in the managerial current. | Broad goals, not clearly delineated, not necessarily related to organizational goals. | Well-defined goals, consistent with organization's needs and values, constantly pursued. |

| | | | |
|---|---|---|---|
| 17. Perseverance, able to stick to a task and see it through regardless of the difficulties encountered. | Loses interest fast. | Sustains interest as long as novelty or stimulation continues. | Keeps looking for ways around obstacles. Maintains optimism out of confidence a solution will be found. |
| 18. Personal organization, has good sense of time. | Poorly organized; doesn't recognize priorities or keep track of information. | Reasonably well-organized. Priorities sometimes questionable. Allows intrusion which eats time. Can answer questions but takes time to dig out information. | Meticulously organized. Makes every minute count. Retrieves information readily, both from own head and organization. |
| 19. Integrity, has a well-established value system, which has been tested in various ways in the past. | Chameleon. Can't really be trusted. Others' opinions have more weight than his or her own. | Ethical, but sometimes rationalizes decisions in favor of bottom line. | Beyond reproach, sometimes almost to point of rigidity. |
| 20. Social responsibility, appreciates the need to assume leadership with respect to that responsibility. | No recognition of executive's public role or wish to fill it. | Recognizes role and wants to fill it out of obligation, but has no significant personal interest in it. | Recognizes responsibility and relishes it as opportunity. Displays active leadership. |

1. *Harvard Business Review*, August/September 1980. Reprinted by permission of Harvard Business Review. Exhibit from "Criteria of Choosing Chief Executives" by Harry Levinson [July/August 1980]. Copyright © 1980 President and Fellows of Harvard College; all rights reserved.

165

I worked with a leader who failed to score high marks on each of these dimensions but yet was very successful as a leader within his organization. Melvin D. was a creative director of a large advertising agency, and he was paid and hired to field the best creative department in the city. Melvin D. knew the talents and abilities of his people very well. He knew that certain employees needed to be motivated to accomplish better work, and others could accomplish excellent work without the over-the-shoulder motivation. It was a real pleasure to see him work and lead his department. He knew how to group his workers together to produce the best work. Some men worked well with women, some worked better with male artists, and some female writers worked better with male artists. It was the job of Melvin D. to team the most compatible people together so that all their talents and abilities were utilized to the fullest extent. By putting the right teams together to go to work for the clients, exceptional work was produced for the good of the company and for everyone concerned within the company. Melvin's ability to motivate and demand quality work helped the company double their sales year after year.

His job became more difficult as the company grew. There were often tremendous amounts of friction and pressure with the company, friction with the other department heads, and friction with the customers in trying to convince them they were getting the best quality of advertising possible. In ten years the company moved from a service company billing about seven million dollars to one billing over fifty million dollars, and Melvin and his staff were an important part of that success story. His creative mind helped the agency win numerous awards, both regional and national. These awards not only gave recognition to the agency, but also reinforced the fine work of the writers and artists. Melvin D. was not good in all twenty dimensions that were listed in Illustration 14, but he made full utilization of the areas in which he excelled. He excelled in number three, intelligence. He was very bright, always drawing on a fountain of experience. He was also articulate and made a good impression on others. He was respected by peers for verbalizing and presenting their problems. You can save a tremendous amount of time if you learn the strengths and weaknesses of the individuals under your supervision. Try to recognize all potential strengths because helping your employees develop will be the key to your success. A leader succeeds if he or she is able to make people work harder. Learn to distinguish between their future potential and their daily performance.

Finally, Melvin D. had an excellent sense of time. The best leaders know the importance of time and mind it very well. Although Melvin D. had a number of clients pulling him apart for work on their own jobs, he was well organized and seemed to make all of his time count for his company as well as his customers. He kept little information on his own. I never saw Melvin filing papers. Instead he would use his secretary for these jobs and he would call on other workers to give him the information he needed to know at that time.

The more you know about your people the easier it will be to relate to them and to be an effective leader. A study of military leadership used a comprehensive test of accuracy. Squad leaders were asked the following questions about each of the ten infantry trainees under them:

1. What is his first name?
2. Has he been on KP during the past week?
3. Has he been on sick call during the past week?
4. Has he had a pass during the past week?
5. What is his rifle qualification score?
6. How many years of schooling has he completed?
7. What was his job before entering the Army?
8. What is his principal hobby or interest?
9. What is his ambition for a future civilian career?

The squad leaders answered similar questions for their trainee sergeant and trainee platoon guide. The correctness of their answers was determined by comparing them with the answers actually given by the trainees, the sergeant, and the guide. The accuracy score was the total number of correct answers. The leaders with the highest accuracy score, incidentally, were the best leaders as judged by the ratings by their trainees, the rating by the sergeant, the rating by the platoon leader, and the score on a standardized leader-reaction test. Good leadership is not being everything to everyone. It means picking your special strengths, talents, and abilities and then building on them to reach your goals. Leaders are paid for doing the difficult things that others find impossible to do. Good leaders use their people well.

# 18
# NOW YOU CAN BEAT
# THE CLOCK

We have discussed numerous techniques, styles, tactics, methods, philosophies, strategies, and ideas both old and new to help you use your time better. Just reading about the methods and ideas will not be enough. You must take the time to break away from the habits you have built over the months, perhaps years, and use these new ideas. Good time management is the proper development of techniques like setting up your priorities each day and sticking to them. Good time management is much like building a winning football team. You must develop it a little more each day.

I overheard two coaches talking about the new football team in the fall. One coach talked about some players who were excellent players while the team was winning, but when the going got tough lost a great deal of steam and enthusiasm. Time management is very similar to this. You will have some days in which the clock will beat you to a pulp. On other days when you set good priorities, stay with those priorities, delegate the jobs that can be handled by others, and guide and manage your time in a way similar to that of a captain running an ocean liner, you can reach your destination.

In every office you will find certain employees who have a natural ability to use time well. Watch their time-management techniques and skills and try to incorporate any that seem appropriate into your own goals and objectives. I recall working with one veteran executive who handled the clock very well because of a wealth of experience in dealing with her secretary and associates. She developed a real understanding of her job and the objectives of the company. She scheduled meetings with her associates and ran the office with one eye on her efficiency and another eye on the clock to watch her time management. But there are many different kinds of time managers.

One time manager is the individual who is called the "too busy" time manager. He or she is always running out of time and ending up with more and more work. Work is always coming into the office to fill up the "in" box, and a large amount is work that could easily be delegated or handled by another department. The work in the "in" box is the subject of much complaining. Why must it be done? How will it be done? What adjustments should be made to do the jobs? The "too busy" time manager becomes nervous about all the work there is to accomplish, and this affects the other people around. This extremely busy style does not permit the other people around you to feel they are a part of the team. Good time management means working well with the team to accomplish your goals and reach your victories. If you feel that the "too busy" time manager description fits you, take the opportunity to slow down, and take an objective look at yourself and your work. What is the most important thing you could be doing right now? What is the "highest payoff" work you could be doing? Do you jump from one thing to another without determining their importance? Do you run your time or do your activities run it? Put more management behind the day-to-day activities.

Another time manager is called the "too lax" time manager. His problem is the complete opposite from that of the preceding manager. This manager is blessed with too much time, not because he completes all the larger, "high payoff" jobs, but because he takes on too many small jobs. He gives the impression that he has caught up with the work, but in reality has plenty of important work to do. This style of time-managing opens the doors for numerous people who want to steal some of your valuable time by discussing their own problems or by helping them pass their time away. The "too lax" time managers like to get together and consume time together, talking about what needs to be done rather than deciding how they can spend their time accomplishing their objectives. If you find yourself falling into this description make an effort to avoid taking all those small jobs that you feel are simple, or the jobs that you feel that you can accomplish in five or ten minutes. What are the responsibilities of your job? Do those quick jobs fit into your job responsibilities? Practice saying "NO" in the mirror and start using it on the job. Why do you have to say "YES" to each request? You will develop a reputation for being a "too lax" time manager and people will treat you as this deserves.

Still another time manager is the "professional" time manager. This one uses time in a very professional manner. He or she has a real time-consciousness, and will not stand for wasting any of that most precious resource—TIME. He values his time, yet he is not so involved in his use of it he becomes a "too busy" or "too lax" time manager. He realizes that he must treat people right for them to treat him right, so his time management style is designed with the professional in mind; he treats others as professionals. The professional knows that dealing with people is a difficult job but he works hard to cooperate with other people. The professional will not simply throw himself into a job; he will plan the job completely before he starts on it. He will decide what people, methods, and materials will be required to do the job. Once this is decided, he will utilize all his resources to the fullest.

He believes in helping people grow within the organization. Why not use the full potentials of all your people? How many people can become administrative assistants, supervisors, junior managers, senior managers, vice-presidents, or even the president of the organization? The mayor of Boston recently sent his employees to a two-day seminar on management skills to help them think more on the managerial level. This seminar helped them meet and better understand each other. The intangible benefits are that the workers now feel that the organization values their services enough to have sent them away to this seminar. The company made a contribution to their career development.

The professional time manager tries to keep up with the latest methods to utilize his time the most effectively, but he will use an idea from a friend, associate, neighbor, salesperson, worker, or anyone else who can show him a better way. He develops a reputation as a person who will not permit a good idea to go to waste. He understands that he can comprehend only so much information and knowledge himself, and to help beat the clock on the wall he must give others the opportunity to better the organization. The professional knows that opening the doors to new ideas within the organization will open another avenue for people to grow around him. As the people grow around him, the ideas and methods they develop will be better and better. The professional time manager creates an environment, to which the people around him respond favorably. This environment is conceived only because the professional is willing to purchase or take the ideas he needs to utilize his time even better. There are too many people in the world of work who will not purchase the products or services they need to do a better job. They spend their time thinking about it or explaining that it is not included in the budget. In my own business experience I have found that certain time mangers, the professionals, will evaluate an idea if it seems to be a better idea. They will purchase the idea and then try it. In accepting the idea, the professional must swallow his pride and accept the fact that the new idea is better than the former way. Progress means determining the best way to do the job and then doing it. The professional opens the gates wide to permit progress to make an entrance.

The professional reaches his success because he presses on to reach the "high payoff" jobs that are essential to the ultimate success of the organization. How does he do it? He uses the aforementioned ideas to handle the jobs and assignments called BOSS and OUR time. The other time managers never seem to move themselves away from BOSS and OUR time. Once they finally reach their MY time, they will find themselves with low energy levels, or faced with only a small amount of time before BOSS time starts again. The professional moves through BOSS and OUR time segments and puts his feet firmly on the ground to conquer the "high payoff" items that are imperative to victory for the organization. The "high payoff" jobs may be the development of the five-year plan for the company, a sales plan, a new promotion plan for the company, purchasing a new machine to increase production, or a job that will give him a payoff in the future.

The professional flows confidently from one job to another making plans and making progress. The reason for his success is his excellent attitude that things will work out for the best. He's a positive thinker and a positive worker and believes in what he is doing. He avoids spending time thinking about why the job will be difficult or will fail. He spends his time telling himself how to do it. He gives himself the pep talk he needs to be successful. He has slogans and signs all over his office to keep him going. Positive thinking is important to the proper execution of time management because it gives you the opportunity to see yourself accomplish the difficult jobs or goals. Positive thinking can help you in many ways. For example, Rocky Bleier, a famous football back for the Pittsburgh Steelers, used his positive thinking to reach his fortune and fame. It didn't come easily. Rocky lost a portion of his foot while serving in combat during the Vietnam War. Once the doctors repaired his foot they told him he would be very lucky if he could ever walk again without the aid of a cane. Rocky, a professional time manager, could not accept this decision. He used the time available to him to consult numerous orthopedic surgeons and endured four operations in three years. With the aid of medical science, training, guts, and believing in himself and his goals, he is now one of only three running backs in the history of the Steelers to rush for over one thousand yards in a season. Rocky serves as an example to his teammates as well as to the youngsters of the country that you can beat adversity. Your positive attitude is the most important defense you can muster to beat your adversity.

The professional is persistent in his drive to reach his goals. Good time management is the zeal to keep on the trail of your goals. You may find that you must change strategies here and there but you should still move in the right direction. The professional is similar to the oil company president who was faced with weeks and months of drilling without striking any oil. Staff meetings were called to determine what action should be taken to remedy this situation. Numerous ideas were presented to the president. He was a professional time manager and took the time to listen to all the ideas and then set them aside to make the final decision himself. The final decision was to continue to look for oil but make a greater effort to reach it. The crew went back to the oil rig, and six weeks later they finally hit the oil for which they had been frantically searching for many months. Asked about the decision to continue, the president remarked, "This oil business is similar to the business of life. Nothing is easy. You work hard and come up with many dry holes. Some people quit when they find the dry holes. Successful people know that to win you must continue to push on. If you drill enough holes long enough and deep enough, you will reap your success." This example of the oil president is a good one because the professional time manager knows that if you quit, you may quit just before you reach success. Your own opportunities might very well be right where you are now, right in your own job, your own business, or organization. Put persistence in your time-management program.

We talked about the water pump as an important prop to use in stressing motivation in accomplishing your goals. Just like the water pump, you must make the necessary effort before the rewards will come to you. It will vary with the time of year. In the summer you might get water without too much effort, but in the winter you must work hard to pump much harder and longer to get the rewards. This is very similar to task of the professional time manager. He or she wants very much to relate well to other people but is aware that he must watch the time management of other people working for him. He wastes few words when he wants to communicate to other workers. He values their ability to use good time management. The professional knows that he is only as good as the people working with him in his department or company. The professional also knows that he cannot please all people, whether workers or customers, and knows that he must reach his own goals. He has the ability to think of big goals and objectives.

The professional has the ability to plan, and plans each day as the most important day of his life. He may want to complete a five-year plan for the company, and if he determines this to be a "high payoff" job he will put this on his "to-do" list as the top priority. Once he has established his number one priority, he will then determine the number two priority, and then number three, and so on. All the priorities are listed in the "to-do" list. When the professional comes into his office the next day for work, he will open his "to-do" book and start on the number one priority. It will be very difficult to stay on the number one without switching to number three or five, but if the number one priority was originally chosen as the top priority, this is the one he will stay on. The professional will work on this priority until it is finished, even if it is six or seven o'clock in the evening and he still isn't finished. The other time managers aforementioned will move from one priority to the next—from number one to number four, back to number three, and so forth, never accomplishing one priority completely. Stay with the number one priority until you finish it. Once that priority is completed, you can go on to number two. Now I realize that while you are working on your number one priority, there is a good possibility that some interruptions will occur that will temporarily take you away from the top priority. The key word here is *temporarily*. One professional time manager in Massachusetts schedules his day's phone calls together so they can be made one after another. By grouping the calls he finds he can choose the time of day when his callers are most likely to be in and avoid the possibility of numerous individual interruptions of his own time. Try to keep the phone conversations to a minimum so that you can get back on the top priority as soon as possible. The professional knows that successful time management takes real discipline, tons of it, to make the best possible use of a commodity: Time. This commodity is limited, yet everyone has the same amount. Once you find yourself using your time in the same manner as the professional, you will then develop a style of time management that will help you finish those difficult-to-accomplish priorities. Once you complete these priorities, you will then develop an inner confidence in yourself that will help you even more in the future. Good time management is knowing the important things you should be doing and then doing them. Good time management is common sense. Avoid trying to be everything to everyone and concentrate on the essential or "high payoff" work. You must learn to delegate more of your routine work as well; by delegating the work you permit the other people within your department to grow and develop on the job. It gives the workers a feeling that you think enough of their abilities to accomplish the work, and makes them reach a little further to accomplish it. Good time management is knowing the major time wasters such as unplanned visitors, unorganized meetings, excessive paperwork, poor communications, socializing, lack of priorities, too little delegation, spreading yourself too thin, the lack of an "I can do it" attitude, and unclear planning. Once you know the time wasters that are problems for you, the next step is to do something about them. Beat your time wasters by making an effort to get around them each day. You can break those habits by objectively looking at your time wasters.

Now is the time for action. You have completed the best manual on time management available today. Now you must put this information into action. Use the forms and ideas right on your job. Don't make the mistake of simply reading about it. This is not enough—you must put into the action the most important management possible: the management of your time, your most precious resource.

# 19
# MOST COMMONLY
# ASKED QUESTIONS
# ON TIME MANAGEMENT

Q. I know I should be doing more "high payoff" jobs, but I find myself moving lower-level priorities up on my list of things to do and never get to the important priorities. What can I do to break this habit?

A. You're avoiding the number one priority or "high payoff" work and to justify this you're taking on the lower-level jobs. You must find the reason why you're avoiding the top items. Do you really want to do them? Do they have a high enough payoff for you? Do you know how to start them? Once you determine that the priority is important enough you will then start it, continue with it, and finally finish it.

Q. I find that too much of my time is spent discussing or listening to the latest gossip in the office. It may start with legitimate business discussions, and then move into "Did you hear about this person?" How can I get out of this habit?

A. You have made an important step in the direction of solving this problem. You have admitted that it *is* a problem. Now the next step is to avoid the people and situations that feed the gossiping. Once you develop a reputation for someone that is too busy to gossip, it will be easier for you to avoid these situations in the future. One time manager broke away from the gossiping group. When he was asked by others about the latest gossip, he would reply,

"Sorry, Jim, but I know nothing about that. I have been so busy with the ABC project that all my time is being consumed by it." The key to avoiding this gossip circle is to break away from it and never feed it again. Once you avoid feeding the circle, the better chance you will have to keep out the time- and energy-consuming gossip circle.

Q. I know what I want to do, and I set up "high payoff" priorities, but I find myself getting interrupted and have trouble getting back to the important priorities. How can I handle the interruptions successfully without getting a reputation of being a grouch?

A. You're asking a very important question. Most successful time managers know the important priorities, work on them, and handle their priorities in such a way that they continue to get the priorities completed. Let's say you're working on the five-year plan for the company, and you're behind the deadline. You must finish it by Friday. John, your assistant, comes into the office holding a sheet of paper. You know he has a question that may take ten to fifteen minutes to answer. Instead of accepting the interruption and losing your train of thought, you might say, "John, I'm in the middle of a project with top priority. Can I drop by your office later?" If you had stopped to work on John's problem, you would have had to stop and start again on your project. Don't make the mistake of reacting to the pressures of the moment. Don't try to please every person who wants to see you. Don't be too free with the most valuable resource you possess—your TIME. Let your secretary know when you have a top priority and need to avoid interruptions in order to finish it. Your secretary will be happy to take some of the routine calls for you, or to determine the purpose of the call, or to handle the call without interrupting you. Your secretary can be an excellent time- and energy-saver for you. Just use him or her to help you. Don't worry about getting the reputation of a grouch. People understand that you cannot just stop whatever job you happen to have in progress and give them immediate attention. Minor interruptions may not hinder your top-priority goals, but when the interruptions get out of hand, you must make some determinations on the value of an open door policy which allows people and situations to steal too much of your time. One time manager tried many different methods to cut down on interruptions, and nothing worked, so he was forced to close his door to get the top-priority work completed on time. He didn't want to use this method, but he found that this method worked for him better than any other method, so he was forced to try it. Another interruption is when people try to give you monkeys (problems other people cannot or will not solve), adding to the items on your "to-do" list. You must manage your interruptions and not let them manage you.

Q. I cannot keep my work area sufficiently clear so that I can find papers and reports when I need them. How can I cut down on this wasted time?

A. Very good question. One time manager spent twenty minutes each week, usually on a Friday afternoon, taking a survey of the papers and information he had accumulated during the week. He would ask himself if he would need this paper in the future. He found that much of the information on his desk was old, and had little, if any, use, so he promptly discarded these papers. He discovered that a secretary in his office also kept a record of certain papers, so he promptly threw his copies away. Take the time to keep your desk clear enough so that you can retrieve information when you need it. Once you start saving papers in large piles, you will not only clutter your desk and your office, but you will find yourself wasting more and more time. Do you have extra furniture and miscellaneous items in your office? If you find that you're not using miscellaneous machines and furniture in your office, remove them to give you the room you need. Once you remove the extra papers and the extra, unused furniture, you will develop a feeling of organization that will help you mind your time even better in the future.

Q. I'm presently working as a technical writer. I know I should set up my jobs as priorities, but I cannot determine which job out of two or three is the most important job.

A. Which job will give you the highest payoff? Which job will help you reach your goals? The important principle in good time management is not to spend excessive time trying to determine the top priority, but to get busy on one of the almost number one priorities. If two or three jobs are equally important, so that you cannot make a quick decision, get busy on any one of them. When you finish the first one, go on to the next one. The most important point here is that you're doing important jobs, and not spending time trying to determine the very highest priority.

Q. If I delegate too much work to my assistant, I'm afraid he or she might want to take my job from me. I want to delegate, but I want to keep my job as well. What do you recommend?

A. Why do you delegate jobs and assignments? Delegation helps give you extra time to do "higher payoff" jobs. It also helps develop and improve the performance of your assistants. You must try to use this extra time to perform jobs and assignments to help you move up in your company or organization. Delegation gives you MY time. Once you move up, it gives your assistant or assistants an opportunity to move into your former position. You have a choice to make here—to delegate and do the extra jobs for your promotion rewards, or to avoid delegating and handle the complete workload yourself, therefore avoiding the extra jobs you need for promotional opportunities. Proper delegation takes practice and time. Once you learn to delegate properly, you will find yourself with the extra time to do the jobs you need to do to succeed.

Q. I find myself losing time because I fail to make decisions, and since I avoid making decisions, I tend to work on lower-priority work to keep me busy. How can I make quick decisions?

A. Too many people find that it's easier to avoid making a decision, than it is to look at all the data and make the decision once and for all. For example, one manager in New Hampshire wanted to purchase a new production machine to increase production capacity and therefore save both time and money for the company. The company knew they needed this machine but delayed the final decision. The decision would save tremendous amounts of time and money but no one would step forward to make the final decision. People are afraid to make a decision because they are afraid they will fail. Finally, the salesman selling the machine helped the company make their decision. He told them if they didn't purchase the machine within thirty days, the price would be seven thousand dollars more. The decision was finally made to purchase the machine. The failure to make decisions robs you of time and energy savings, and fills you with guilt feelings about not stepping forward to make the decision. You might find that the most important decision you could make is to get your priorities in order, and to get busy on the top priority that will give you the "high payoff" results in the future. You might want to make a decision to spend more of your extra time in that side business you want to build, or to spend more time on the golf course, or spend more time with your family or friends. Your decision must keep YOU in mind. Determine how this decision will help you save time, make more money, attain that promotion, increase your sales, make your company more productive and competitive, or give you the raise you deserve. When you can vividly see the benefits you will receive you will have more impetus to make the decisions. Once you develop confidence in making decisions, it will be much easier in the future. Make the decision to make the important decisions.

Q. I value my personal time. How can I get more of the MY time you discussed earlier?

A. The goal of this time-management book is not only to help my readers get more important work completed on the job, but to have time left over to use for themselves, their MY time. How do you want to spend your MY time: writing, painting, golfing, skiing, reading, spending time with your family, collecting coins, collecting stamps, playing tennis or softball? Once you decide on how you want to spend your MY time, you must determine how many hours per day or week you need and make every attempt to use them. Do you have anyone to share some of your lawn-mowing or handy projects at home? Can you delegate some of those chores that you assumed alone for so many months or perhaps years? Be SELFISH; think of yourself; get other people, machines, or newer methods to free up your MY time. If you can spare some time for golf on Monday, take it, and you will find it easier to recover the time on Tuesday. You must take advantage of every hour, or half hour, or quarter hour you can get your hands on, to build up your MY time. You gave up your MY time on a gradual basis, whether it was your career, your family, or other obligations and now you must gradually get this time back for yourself. Once you find that you can get some time for yourself, you will then develop confidence to get even more time in the future. Take the necessary time to please the most important person: YOU.

Q. The priorities in my office change quickly. I'd like to set priorities but find myself moving from one to another. What can I do?

A. You said the priorities in your office change—that might mean your boss is changing his or her priorities. Why let the changes affect the way you handle your priorities? Stay on the most important priority until it's finished, then move to the next highest priority. Mind your time. Time is money. Money is time.

GOOD LUCK

## Date Due

| | | | |
|---|---|---|---|
| JUL 2 8 1987 | | | |
| AUG 1 1 1988 | | | |
| OCT 1 8 1989 | | | |
| NOV 3 0 1989 | | | |
| JUL 1 7 1990 | | | |
| FEB 1 2 1991 | | | |
| OCT 7 1991 | | | |
| | | | |
| | | | |
| | | | |
| | | | |

DISCARD